Contents

Tables

Illustrations

Foreword

This third report in IFPRI's Food Policy Review series appears at a time when the issue of food price instability has reemerged as an important one. The long-run declining trend in real cereal prices in the world market and large food surpluses in most exporting countries drew international attention away from the problem of food price instability until recently. Sharp price hikes in the world cereal market in 1995, however, have led to renewed interest in price stabilization measures, especially in poor developing countries with limited capacity to meet rising import costs.

This review summarizes the current state of knowledge regarding the theory of price stabilization and its expected benefits. It stresses the need for extending the frontiers of the analytical framework to include macroeconomic, dynamic, and developmental aspects of price stabilization. Under the prevailing restrictive microlevel analysis of risk aversion, focusing on maximization of utility, the benefits of price stabilization are found to be modest, under varying assumptions relating to magnitudes of risk aversion.

Islam and Thomas focus on five Asian developing countries with wide experience in food price stabilization policies. They evaluate the causes and consequences of instability in rice and wheat prices, distinguishing between import-substituting and exporting countries. In explaining why the degree of price stability achieved differed from country to country, they consider differences in the role of private trade in different country's cereal markets, the efficiency of the public buffer stock agencies, and their access to financial resources.

As countries raise their per capita income levels, diversify their economies, and liberalize their foreign trade and domestic output markets in the aftermath of the Uruguay Round, as the world cereal markets are liberalized and surplus stocks are reduced, they rethink the objectives of price stabilization and the appropriate measures for reducing the range of fluctuations in cereal prices. This review will stimulate discussion and contribute to the debate on the pros and cons of food price stabilization among policymakers and analysts at national and international levels.

Per Pinstrup-Andersen
Director General

Acknowledgments

We acknowledge the many helpful comments received on an earlier draft of the manuscript from David Bigman, now at the World Bank, and Keijiro Otsuka of IFPRI. We received valuable assistance on sources of data and previous studies on price policies in the selected countries from Francesco Goletti, Sohail Malik, and Mercedita Agcaoili-Sombilla. We greatly benefited from numerous discussions on the subject with Romeo Bautista and Raisuddin Ahmed at IFPRI.

We are deeply grateful to Vickie Lee for her patient and careful assistance through many revisions in preparing this manuscript for publication.

Nurul Islam
Saji Thomas

1

Summary

S hould countries allow foodgrain prices to fluctuate freely or should they intervene to stabilize domestic prices? Traditional welfare analysis at the micro level concludes that economic benefits of price stabilization for consumers or producers, in general, tend to be small unless great importance is placed on risk aversion. In the simulation exercises undertaken in this study of micro level benefits to producers, which incorporate currently available estimates of risk aversion within an analytical framework based on the maximization of expected utility, price stabilization policies do not seem to yield large benefits. Analysts have questioned the appropriateness of the use of this framework and the treatment of risk aversion within the framework in view of the high priority that farmers in developing countries attach to economic security to avoid disaster and achieve a subsistence level of income. The macroeconomic benefits of price stabilization, including concerns for social and political stability, have not been adequately explored. Nevertheless, while the debate among analysts goes on, policymakers in many developing countries continue to pursue the objective of foodgrain price stabilization using different instruments with varying degrees of success and costs.

This report surveys the most salient arguments for and against foodgrain price stabilization in developing countries. In analyzing the problem, it focuses on the operational aspects of the policies of five Asian developing countries—Bangladesh, Indonesia, Pakistan, the Philippines, and Thailand—which over several decades have had considerable experience in alleviating the instability of foodgrain prices arising from fluctuations in world prices or domestic production. This analysis concentrates on principal foodgrains such as rice and wheat and distinguishes between exporting and importing countries because they involve different implementation problems as well as additional objectives.

All five countries sought to moderate real price fluctuations over the seasons in a year and from year to year. However, this objective was pursued along with a number of interrelated objectives. These include ensuring a floor or an incentive price to producers and a ceiling price to consumers in order to protect them, especially the urban consumers, from a high or sudden rise in food prices; attainment of increased self-sufficiency in foodgrains and the highest possible foreign exchange earnings through maintenance of high and stable export prices. Price stabilization per se, in the sense of reducing the variability of real prices by a certain percentage, was not the sole objective.

None of the countries followed a policy in which floor and ceiling prices were fixed around a target price. Nor did they aim to reduce price variability by a certain percentage. Ceiling or ration prices were determined ad hoc depending on criteria such as poor consumers' income, urban wages, procurement prices, and costs of storage, distribution, and marketing. Procurement prices were determined based on costs of production, prices of competing crops, major input prices, and border prices.

The most commonly used stabilization schemes in developing countries were either buffer stocks or a combination of buffer stocks and trade policies. Countries did not resort to policies such as crop insurance or futures markets, which are primarily designed to reduce or spread the risks of price fluctuations for producers. Problems such as adverse selection, moral hazard, and simultaneous crop failures detracted from the feasibility of crop insurance schemes. The lack of experience with futures in the domestic markets in the developing countries with inadequately organized private commodity exchanges, especially for small farmers, made them difficult to implement.

For successful operation of public stocks combined with trade policy for price stabilization, the experience of Asian countries provides a few lessons:

- The buffer stock agency must have assured and flexible access to financial resources.
- The buffer stock agency must be able to regulate its timing of purchases and sales in order to influence decisions by traders and producers. Also the public agency must conduct market operations on an adequate scale and in an efficient and timely manner to prevent counterspeculation by private traders.
- The management of public stocks requires expertise in rolling over stocks in order to avoid spoilage in long-term storage.
- If public stock reduces or substitutes for private storage, the success of the public effort will be compromised. The private sector should be able to function unhindered in storing, marketing, and processing of foodgrains. This includes not only traders and marketing intermediaries but also farmers who hold surplus stocks.

In meeting these criteria, Indonesia was relatively more successful than the other countries. The actual operating costs of price stabilization were often not known since the food agencies performed other functions unrelated to the price stabilization policy.

The long-run trend in both the border and wholesale prices of rice was downward only in Bangladesh and Thailand; for Basmati rice in Pakistan, the trend in both the border and wholesale prices was upward. In the Philippines, the border price went up and the wholesale price went down. In Indonesia, there was no significant trend in the border price, while there was an upward trend in the wholesale price.

There was no systematic pattern over time in the way in which the wholesale price of rice moved in relation to its border price, as shown by a comparison of three-year moving averages during the 1960s or 1970s to the 1980s. There was a reduction, in general, in the year-to-year variability in production and prices during the 1980s as a whole, compared with the 1970s, in several countries, even though there was no consistent pattern of changes in the five-year averages of price variability.

There was no consistent pattern of relationship between intercountry differences in the ratio of procurement to output and intercountry differences in price variability. The flexibility and timeliness of procurement operations were crucial to the outcome.

In most cases, the variability of domestic prices was lower than the variability of border prices, in some cases substantially lower. Interventions to stabilize domestic prices did not constitute a major factor in determining the nominal protection rate. Even if the real domestic price remained unchanged over time, changes in the nominal protection rate would have occurred due to changes in the real exchange rate and the real border price.

There has been a general trend in recent years toward privatization and liberalization of the input and output markets in developing countries. Also, there is a search for noninterventionist and market-oriented measures. In this context, countries may seek to reduce wide or significant variations in food prices by smoothing out fluctuations around a long-run trend in world prices so that comparative cost considerations are not sacrificed. Taxes and subsidies will be required on imports or exports, as the case may be, to implement a price band policy, which should be flexible, changing in response to underlying supply and demand conditions. The width of the band with a fixed ceiling and floor around a target price should be wide enough to leave adequate incentive for private traders to hold stocks and to play a stabilizing role.

In view of the time lag involved either in procuring imports or selling exports, variations in prices cannot always be exclusively dealt with by trade policy without recourse to public stocks to tide the country over the time lag, especially when there is a sudden or acute food shortage.

As self-sufficiency and per capita incomes improve, concern about food price fluctuations per se decreases. In countries where the effects of a sudden price rise on the poorest consumers or an unforeseen collapse in producers' prices could be severe, the provision of a "safety net" for the poorest through assistance programs such as feeding programs, subsidized targeted food distribution, or food-for-work programs should be considered. Public procurement as a temporary measure at minimum floor prices is another possible safety net.

As the developing economies open up to international price signals under the Uruguay Round agreement, these trade measures will involve a departure from or an exception to the new rules of the game. How much world food price stability there will be in the future is uncertain. While decreased protectionism reduces price instability, it also reduces surplus output and hence stocks, especially in developed, exporting countries. The developing countries have a 10-year period to adjust to the new regime. As the promised new round of agricultural trade negotiations gets under way in 1999, they may renegotiate the need for trade measures to meet food price instability.

2

Introduction

Few countries allow the market prices of foodgrains to fluctuate freely without some form of intervention. This was true historically and it is true today, in both developed and developing countries. The question of whether price stabilization of foodgrains is desirable has been debated extensively in the economic literature. Some argue that the benefits of price stabilization are small, while others contend that even if there are benefits, the costs of implementing such a policy outweigh the possible benefits. While the debate among analysts goes on, policymakers in many developing countries are pursuing the objective of foodgrain price stabilization and using different instruments to this end with varying degrees of success and at different costs.

In recent years, questions have been raised not only about the rationale for public intervention in foodgrain prices through public participation in production and trade and its direct and indirect costs, but also about the extensive controls and regulations used to influence marketing, distribution, and prices in many countries. The objectives often include, along with the stabilization of foodgrain prices, the promotion of domestic self-sufficiency in foodgrains and redistribution of income or food among different income and occupational groups. The efficiency lost through misallocation of resources, resulting from considerable divergence between world and domestic prices of food and agricultural products, is increasingly recognized. Market reforms and liberalization policies seek to reduce or eliminate such losses, but support for stabilization of food prices, as distinguished from a policy that perpetuates the long-term divergence of domestic prices from world prices, continues to be strong in developing countries. It therefore is pertinent at this stage to explain the debate, to survey the most salient arguments for and against foodgrain price stabilization in developing countries, and to analyze the experience of a few Asian developing countries that have sought to achieve a degree of foodgrain price stabilization in recent decades.

Chapters 3 to 5 of this review examine first, the analytics of the major aspects of price stabilization as contained in the mainstream literature. Second, several operational aspects of policies widely adopted for stabilization of foodgrain price variability, arising from either domestic production fluctuations or variations in world prices in an open economy, are discussed. All stabilization policies, whether based on trade or buffer stocks, involve direct financial costs and indirect spillover effects for monetary, fiscal, and foreign exchange policies. Third, alternative policies that are designed to protect producers against price instability rather than to reduce the instability of market prices are examined. They relate to the futures markets and crop insurance.

Chapters 6 to 9 concentrate on the experiences of the five Asian countries (Bangladesh, Indonesia, Pakistan, the Philippines, and Thailand), particularly regarding the operational aspects of the price stabilization policies that are presented in the earlier chapters. They analyze the objectives of price stabilization and other related objectives of the countries and the design and implementation of their price stabilization policies. These policies are often used as part of a wider policy effort to affect the level of food prices in relation to their world prices as well as the prices of other commodities, including nonfood and nonagricultural commodities. The analysis concentrates on the principal foodgrains in each country, rice or wheat or both (although wheat is important in only a few of the selected countries). It distinguishes between importing and exporting countries because the objectives and implementation problems differ. The review also examines the relative role of trade, including taxes on imports and exports and the holding of domestic buffer stocks by a public agency. It looks at criteria for the determination of prices by the foodgrain agency for public procurement from producers and public distribution to consumers.

Chapters 10 and 11 of this review assess the consequences of price stabilization policies—their impact on the variability of foodgrain prices across countries and over time. They also quantify the microeconomic benefits of foodgrain stabilization, following the methodology discussed in Chapters 3 to 5, and examine the changes over time in the degree of price variability and the reasons for these changes, including changes in technology and cropping patterns. They compare the degree of price variability in the past as a result of policies pursued in the respective countries, on the one hand, with the price variability that would have occurred in the absence of stabilization policies and under a regime of free trade, on the other. They consider the variability of prices that would have prevailed under a different policy, such as the "band rule" (an upper and lower band imposed on the variability of prices). They also briefly summarize recent developments in price stabilization policies in the selected countries and assess the outlook for the future.

This review surveys the policies followed in the five selected countries, rather than presenting detailed case studies of price policy in the individual countries, based on a collection of new primary data on the producers and consumers of foodgrains. It draws heavily on available country studies and occasionally supplements them with new data and analysis. How does the present review differ from other syntheses or surveys that have been attempted in the past? The construction of relevant data that is consistent and comparable over a number of years and countries from a multiplicity of not-so-readily-available sources was an extremely time-consuming and labor-intensive enterprise. It includes data such as time series of wholesale, retail, border, procurement, and release prices as well as the amount of procurement and public distribution. For example, border prices for importing countries are not based on the exporting country's f.o.b. prices plus an estimated margin of c.i.f., as is done in most country studies; in the present study, they are based on actual import prices. The quantitative picture that emerges is not the same as in earlier studies where comparative analysis was available. Moreover, the available country studies often do not cover the same aspects of policy or the same time period, and they are seldom current. In most cases, conclusions based on noncomparable data were not compatible. Past studies often did not follow the same methodology for computing long-run trends and degree of variability of prices as in this study.

Few comparative or synthetic studies were available, and those that were did not cover the same set of issues. Although the studies on Indonesia and the Philippines covered only two of the five countries analyzed in the current report (Dawe and Timmer 1991; Timmer 1988 and 1989a), they were the most comparable with the present study. They were limited, however, to a period shorter than the present one and mainly focused on three aspects of stabilization policy: (1) size of buffer stock, (2) timing and financial flexibility in the operation of buffer stocks, and (3) the degree of price stability achieved. The present study spans a wider number of issues on a consistent and comparable set of data over a comparable and a longer period. In addition, it seeks to estimate or quantify the benefits of stabilization. The other studies of Asian price policies that could be considered partially comparable with the present study—for example, Asian Development Bank (1988), Bigman (1982, 1985, 1988), and Sicular (1989)—did not cover all the countries included in the present study. Some focus on long-term aspects rather than short-term stability (except when analysis of the food subsidy program is undertaken), and they treat at length the allocative efficiency losses involved in price distortion rather than issues of price variability. They also deal with the issue of the transfer of resources between agriculture and the rest of the economy, which is caused either by discrimination against the food sector or by protection of the sector against foreign competition. Again, none of the studies deal with wheat: only rice is covered. Nor do these studies examine how the objectives, characteristics, and techniques of price stabilization differ between the food-exporting and the food-importing countries. The analysis of recent changes in price stabilization policies and objectives is also a new feature found only in the present study.

3

A Brief Summary of the Analytics of Price Stabilization

This chapter briefly summarizes current thinking on price stabilization. The objectives, as well as the pros and cons, of price stabilization are analyzed from the viewpoint of both producers and consumers. Micro issues are considered as well as macro and economywide issues. A large number of authors have surveyed this field: comprehensive studies by Newbery and Stiglitz (1981), Kanbur (1984), Bigman (1982, 1985), Wright and Williams (1991), and Classens (1993), to mention only a few. This chapter is not intended to be an exhaustive survey of literature of all the analytical issues. Only a few points considered most germane to the issue of food price stabilization in developing countries are discussed here, and they focus on only a few staples. Issues relating to the stabilization of prices of agricultural raw material exports in world markets and stabilization of domestic prices of agricultural exports are not covered.

Earlier works on price stabilization (Oi 1961; Waugh 1944; Massel 1969) were partial equilibrium analyses. Their models were mirror images of each other for producers and consumers. Both models assume that producers are risk neutral, supply is stochastic, both supply and demand disturbances are additive, buffer stocks are costless to hold and administer, agents are risk neutral, trade in grains is free, and prices are stabilized perfectly. Supply adjusts instantaneously to a change in price. These models have the general form

$$q^d = a - bP + u, \text{ and}$$

$$q^s = c + dP + \gamma,$$

where u and γ are the stochastic disturbances and q^d and q^s are the quantities demanded and supplied, respectively. P is the price.

Oi (1961) considers the producer in a perfectly competitive market with a stable marginal cost curve and a profit function that is convex in prices.

By construction, since the profit function is convex in prices, the expected profit of a wider dispersion of prices (P_1^* and P_2^*) is greater than that of a narrow dispersion of prices (P_1 and P_2). Thus, the expected profits will be higher, the greater is the variance of prices.

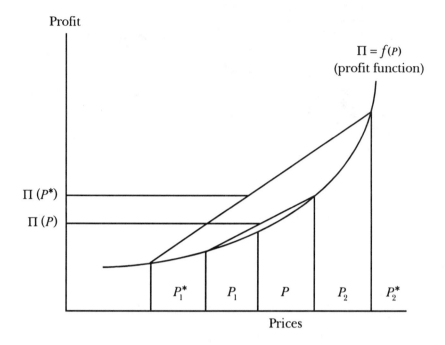

Waugh (1944) makes a parallel analysis of expected utility and prices for consumers and concludes that consumers gain from price instability. It has been argued that when price variations occur due to variations in supply, let us say in food commodities, given a downward sloping curve, consumers gain from instability because they buy more when prices are low and buy less when prices are high. They store when prices are low and consume stored commodities when prices go up or buy less expensive food. In these circumstances, price stabilization reduces consumer welfare by preventing consumers from increasing consumption levels when harvests are good and reducing consumption levels when harvests are poor. The size of the welfare loss is proportional to the price elasticity of demand. While Oi and Waugh each look separately at the impact on producers and consumers, Massel (1969) integrates the results to consider the welfare effects of price stabilization in a model containing both producers and consumers. This can be summarized by considering the demand and supply curves in the figure on page 9.

The producer's surplus at different prices is as follows:

at P_2, $a + b + c + d + f$;

at P_1, f;

at P, $a + b + f$, where $P = \dfrac{P_1 + P_2}{2}$.

It is assumed that both P_1 and P_2 have an equal probability of occurrence so that $Prob\ (P_1) = Prob(P_2) = 0.5$. Thus, if price is P_2 instead of P, then the producers' gain is $c + d$. However, if price is P_1, then the

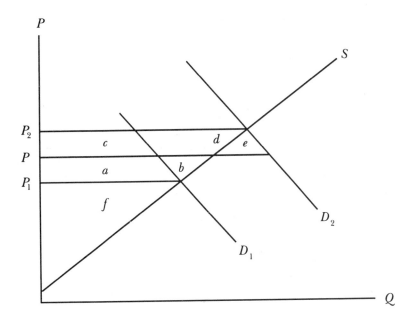

producers' loss is $a + b$. Thus price stabilization reduces the expected value of the producer surplus by $\frac{1}{2}(c + d - a - b)$. Assuming an upward sloping curve $c + d > a + b$, price stabilization leads to reduced expected profits.

Massel (1969) further integrates consumer surplus and producer surplus to measure the overall welfare gains. In particular, reducing the price from P_2 to P involves a gain to consumers of $c + d + e$ and a loss to producers of $c + d$, yielding a net gain of e. Raising the price from P_1 to P benefits producers by $a + b$ and costs the consumers only a, thus resulting in a net gain of b. Overall, therefore, consumers and producers jointly gain $b + e$; thus assuming costless storage, there is an overall welfare gain from price stabilization.

Even though the above models serve as an introduction to the basic welfare analysis of price stabilization, the results depend on the assumptions underlying the model, many of which do not hold in the real world. First, though additive disturbance terms are used in the supply and demand model to simplify the analysis, the real world agricultural market is better described in multiplicative disturbance terms. An additive risk in the supply model is characterized as

$$q = f(x) + \widetilde{\theta}; \quad E(\widetilde{\theta}) = 0; \quad \text{and} \quad \text{var } \widetilde{\theta} = \sigma^2,$$

where $\widetilde{\theta}$ is a random variable for external factors like weather or disease and $E(\widetilde{\theta})$ is the expected value of $\widetilde{\theta}$. It is assumed that risk destroys a constant amount regardless of the size of the total crop. For example, disease wipes out a limited area of the crop independent of the total area. Thus, there will occur parallel shifts in the demand or supply model under additive disturbances.

On the other hand, a multiplicative risk is characterized by

$$q = \tilde{\theta}\, f(x), \text{ where } E\tilde{\theta} = 0, \text{ var } \tilde{\theta} = \sigma^2.$$

The multiplicative risk term in the supply function accounts for the fact that the area devoted to a particular crop is usually price responsive, where actual supply is area times the stochastic yield. Thus, rain at harvest time leads to spoilage, which is a constant fraction of the crop, regardless of its size, or disease affects a fraction of the crop (which is more realistic than is implied by additive disturbance). Thus, if the elasticity of demand and supply curves change, the gains to producers and consumers could also change, as pointed out by Turnovsky (1976).

Second, the Oi and Massel models also assume that producers and consumers can modify their production and consumption decisions at no cost. Although the Oi, Waugh, and Massel models assume that producers and consumers have perfect foresight regarding future prices, in reality, they must base their decisions on their expectations about future prices. Once supply is made to depend on the expected price level, the autoregressive properties of the stochastic disturbances become important in determining the welfare gains from price stabilization. Thus both the lag in the mechanism of expectation formation and the autoregressive properties of the random disturbance determine the distribution of gains and losses.

Third, the traditional model assumes linear demand and supply models. However, when nonlinearities are introduced in the model, the distribution of gains from price stabilization changes. It is not easy to quantify the benefits of stabilization. In this case the stabilized price at which the buffer stock is self-liquidating is no longer the arithmetic mean price. One cannot conclude anything about whether the stabilized price is greater or smaller than the expected price (the arithmetic mean price). One can illustrate this for the consumer's benefit as follows.

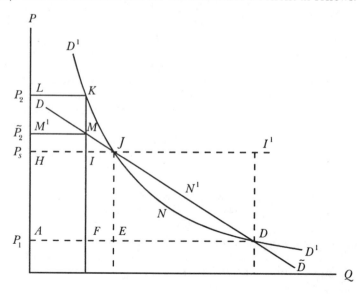

The nonlinear demand curve is shown by D^1D^1. (The linear demand curve is DD.) It is assumed that the prices fluctuate between P_1 and P_2 due to shifts in supply (vertical supply curve) but that price is stabilized at P_s by buffer stock authority. When the price is stabilized at P_s, preventing it from rising to P_2, the consumers gain $HJKL$, an area larger than the area under the linear demand curve $HJMM^1$. When the price is P_1, after stabilization to $\overline{P}_s$, the consumers lose because of higher prices, an amount equal to $ADNJH$. The net benefits could be positive or negative because whether the losses are greater or smaller than the gains depends to a large extent on the position of the stabilized price, P_s, between the lower price, P_1, and the higher price, P_2. Depending on the position of P_s and the degree of nonlinearity or curvature of the demand curve, losses ($ADNJH$) could be greater or smaller than gains ($HJKL$).

Fourth, the traditional model assumes that individuals are indifferent to risk, or that the commodity under discussion forms a sufficiently small part of total producer and consumer surplus so that a change in price leaves the marginal utility unchanged. This is unlikely to hold in the context of price instability and uncertainty for commodities like food. When risk aversion is not taken into account (or if individuals are risk neutral), the gains from stabilization are underestimated. The risk faced by farmers falls as price instability is reduced.

Fifth, the traditional model assumes that there is no linkage between product markets. For instance, if the supply of the commodity under consideration rises because of a fall in price instability (and thus risk), then the real incomes of consumers rise, and they buy more of other commodities, too. Thus, total utility is a function of both the good whose price is stabilized and other goods they consume.

Since the early work of Oi, Waugh, and Massel, many others have attempted to extend the basic model by relaxing the assumptions made in the traditional model. Turnovsky (1974) used the multiplicative risk instead of additive risk along with nonlinear demand and supply functions. It is the slopes rather than their relative position that matters in this context. He concludes that in the additive case the desirability of price stabilization depends on the source of price instability: whether price fluctuations occur as a result of supply or demand fluctuations. But in the case of multiplicative risk, it depends on the deterministic components of demand and supply rather than the stochastic disturbance term. Thus, if one group benefits from price stabilization, it will do so whether the source of the stochastic disturbance is on the demand side or the supply side. The distribution of the benefits is indeterminate and depends on the elasticity of demand and supply. If the demand is more elastic than the supply, then producers gain from price stabilization, but if supply is more elastic than demand, then consumers gain. For example, with a log-linear demand and supply function (which is a case of multiplicative risk), producers gain if and only if the elasticity of demand is greater than unity, and consumers always gain regardless of the elasticity of demand and supply.

Turnovsky (1979) further extended the basic model by allowing supply to depend on the expected price level (that is, farmers do not have perfect foresight). The model is specified as

$$S = a + bP_t^* + v_t, \text{ and}$$

$$D = c - dP_t + u_t,$$

Farmers are assumed to have adaptive price expectations, defined as

$$P_t^* - P_{t-1}^* = \gamma(P_{t-1} - P_{t-1}^*),$$

where $0 \leq \gamma \leq 1$ and $b, d \geq 0$. P_t^* is the price expected to prevail at time t. Once supply is made to depend on the expected price level, the autoregressive properties of the stochastic disturbances become important in determining the welfare gains from stabilization.

Using the linear model (as shown above) with adaptive expectations, it is evident that producers experiencing uncertainty due to random fluctuations in demand can either gain or lose from stabilization. The likelihood of benefiting varies inversely with the autoregressive parameters. If the u_t is negatively correlated or not at all correlated with γ, then producers gain; if u_t is positively and strongly correlated with γ, then producers lose. The reason for these differences in distribution of gains is that supply is now a function of previous prices. With demand being subject to stochastic shifts, these prices become random, and random elements in demand induce random shifts in supply. The parameters are important. If demand is infinitely elastic ($d \rightarrow \infty$), then all gains are equal to zero. If $\gamma \rightarrow 0$, so that expectations are slow to adjust, all the gains from stabilization go to consumers. Turnovsky also finds that the total expected gains when price expectations are adaptively formed are at least as great as when supply depends upon actual prices. With rational expectations, it is concluded, however, that producers cannot gain from price stabilization in the case of demand fluctuations; in other words, they are better off being able to exploit the information available to them (this is in contrast to the case of adaptive expectations). The total gains from stabilization are at least as great as those obtained under the assumption of perfect supply flexibility. With negatively correlated disturbances, nothing conclusive can be said, and for independently distributed disturbances, gains are equal.

In this context, it is appropriate to explain the difference between adaptive and rational expectations. In an adaptive expectations model the forecast price for the current year is a geometric weighted average of past observed prices. It is given as

$$P_t^e = \lambda P_{t-1} + (1 - \lambda) P_{t-1}^e,$$

where P_t^e is the expected price in time, and P_{t-1} is the actual price in time $t-1$. λ is a constant and lies between $0 \leq 1$. According to the adaptive rule,

$$P_t^e - P_{t-1}^e = \lambda(P_{t-1} - P_{t-1}^e).$$

Thus, farmers compare last year's forecast price P_{t-1}^e with the actual market price P_{t-1} and adjust this year's forecast to reduce the discrepancy by some fraction of λ. Thus,

$$P_t^e = \lambda P_{t-1} + (1 - \lambda) P_{t-1}^e .$$

In a rational expectations model, the farmer forecasts the expected price at time (t) using past observations on price (p), own output (q), and other external factors (s). Thus, the forecast price (P_t^e) is given as

$$P_t^e = t (P_{t-1} , P_{t-2} , \ldots P_{t-n} ; q_{t-2} , \ldots q_{t-n} , s_{t-1}).$$

The most comprehensive treatment of commodity price stabilization to date is the seminal work by Newbery and Stiglitz (1981). They formulate a model to quantify the benefits to producers and consumers in terms of expected utility (which depends on the mean variance of prices and income) rather than in terms of producer and consumer surplus. The benefit of price stabilization to, say, producers is estimated from the point of view of its effects on their income or consumption variability. Price variability is not the same as variability of income, which is the joint result of variability of output and that of price.

In fact, producers are concerned with price stabilization only to the extent that it stabilizes their income. In some cases, price stabilization actually enhances income variability. Whether stabilization increases or decreases the variance of income depends on whether the price elasticity of demand is less than or greater than 0.5 in absolute terms. When the price elasticity of demand is greater than 0.5 but less than 1.0 and supply fluctuation is the cause of price fluctuations, then price stabilization may destabilize income (Newbery and Stiglitz 1981, 27). This is because when demand is elastic, shortfalls in supply are followed by a less than proportionate increase in prices, and stabilization of prices increases income variability. But, when the demand is inelastic, shortfalls in supply are compensated by a more than proportionate rise in prices, and price stabilization decreases the variability of income. Thus, price stabilization destabilizes income if the price elasticity of demand is between 0.5 and 1.0. In most of the developing countries, the price elasticity of demand for food crops is likely to be less than 0.5; thus price stabilization will lead to income stabilization. The adverse effects on producers of a price slump in a good harvest season may be much larger than the beneficial effects when harvests are poor and prices are high. For example, in Bangladesh, the adverse effect of a fall in price in the absence of stabilization was found to be 47 percent higher than the positive effect for surplus farmers during a rise in prices (Ahmed and Bernard 1989). Moreover, the variability of income of producers is not the same thing as variability of their consumption; it is possible to smooth consumption over time through recourse to the credit market. However, producers face imperfect capital markets: they may be unable to cash in on these gains. Therefore, they may never reach the "long run" because they may go bankrupt if prices drop drastically as demand declines.[1]

Moreover, the probable gains that may accrue to producers from price instability—by producing more when the price is high and producing less when the price is low—are not likely to be realized. For example, there is a lag between the time when an increase in supply is needed to meet a shift in demand and when the actual increase occurs. Even if producers know with certainty that next period's price is going to be sufficiently high to induce an increase in production, costs of adjustments in input structure may not enable them to adjust their output to desired levels.

Price instability imposes costs on consumers who have to readjust their consumption and budget in response to a change in the relative price. This imposes a welfare loss on consumers to the extent that they place value on the avoidance of transaction costs. Consumers, especially poor consumers, are obliged to look for substitute commodities, including inferior substitutes, when prices rise. The search for an inferior substitute not only involves transaction costs but also reduces utility.

Newbery and Stiglitz (1981) make significant departures from the earlier approaches to price stabilization. They find that under different assumptions than the one stated in the traditional models used by Oi, Waugh, and Massel, welfare gains to producers and consumers may differ both qualitatively and quantitatively in the short and long runs. Newbery and Stiglitz use a simple long-run rational expectations equilibrium model, where the producers adjust their output in response to changes in risk. The price stabilization scheme changes the expected marginal utility of production, which induces a change in the output level. The model assures that all producers are identical, grow only one crop (single-market analysis), and have constant relative risk aversion.

First, Newbery and Stiglitz distinguish between different types of price expectations—adaptive and rational, as opposed to actual prices. Supply is determined by the expected price, wherein the farmer forecasts the expected price using information on past prices and output and other information relevant to the future (rational expectations). This is in contrast to the conventional approach of Massel (1969), wherein producers make their decisions based on the actual selling prices and adjust instantaneously to any change in price.

Second, they dispense with the problem of relying on linear demand and supply functions to calculate producer and consumer surplus.

---

[1]The experience with public financial institutions in providing credit to farmers through either loan targeting or through subscribed interest rates has been disappointing. An effective way of providing credit, in view of problems arising from asymmetric information, limitations in monitoring of credit use, and enforcement of repayment, has often eluded the grasp of public financial institutions. Although new forms of financing to get around the imperfections of financial markets have recently been devised, the effects of price fluctuations on farmers' ability to repay and hence on the variability of financial institutions poses additional challenges.

Instead, they use the "expected utility" hypothesis, which focuses on producer revenue for producers and consumer income for consumers.

Third, they assume shifts in supply and demand functions by incorporating multiplicative risk in the demand and supply schedules.

Fourth, they include risk aversion in the estimation of benefits of stabilization. The concept and quantitative magnitude of risk aversion are discussed in Newbery and Stiglitz (1981) and Binswanger (1980). After analyzing various experimental studies that were undertaken to measure risk aversion or premium expressed as a percentage of current income, Newbery and Stiglitz conclude that few individuals have risk aversion levels much above 2. In Binswanger's estimate, the magnitude varies between 0.32 and 1.74. Most individuals are risk averse and react to fluctuations in income.

The concept of risk aversion (aversion to income loss) is explained by Newbery and Stiglitz in the following way. Let $U(y)$ be the utility function, where U is concave and expected utility is associated with a random variation y, for income.

$$\bar{y} = \begin{cases} \bar{y} + \partial & \text{with probability of } \frac{1}{2} \\ \bar{y} - \partial & \text{with probability of } \frac{1}{2} \end{cases},$$

where $\bar{y}$ is sure income.

Therefore, expected utility $= E\,U(\bar{y}) = \frac{1}{2}\{U(\bar{y}+\partial) + U(\bar{y}-\partial)\}$. It is halfway between two utility levels. And with a concave utility function, expected utility is less than $U(\bar{y})$, that is, utility associated with $\bar{y}$, or sure income.

Various studies indicate that effects of risk on the producers can be represented as a negative shifter on the supply function, indicating that, all things being equal, the higher the risk in production of a certain product, the smaller the output. A firm facing uncertain prices for its products and selecting its output so as to maximize the expected utility from profits assumes that the firm has a continuous, differentiable, and concave utility function $U(\pi)$, where $\pi = P_x - C(x)$ is the firm's profit and $C(x)$ is its cost function. First order conditions for profit maximization imply that

$$E\{U^1(\pi)[P - C^1(x)]\} = 0.$$

But

$$E\{U^1(\pi)[P - C^1(x)]\} = E[U^1(\pi)][\bar{P} - C^1(x)] + \text{cov}\{U^1(\pi)[P - C^1(x)]\}$$

where $\bar{P} = E(P)$. Rearranging, it can be written

$$\bar{P} + \frac{\text{cov}[U^1(\pi)P]}{E[U^1(\pi)]} = C^1(x).$$

For risk-adverse firms, cov $[U^1(\pi)P] < 0$ firms, whereas $U^1(\pi) > 0$. Hence,

$$\frac{\text{cov}[U^1(\pi)P]}{E[U^1(\pi)]} \text{ is} < 0.$$

The firm therefore equates marginal cost to a price lower than the mean price in order to determine its optimum level of output. The difference between that price and the mean price represents the risk premium that rises with an increase in the degree of the firm's risk aversion. The optimum level of output of a risk-averse firm will be less than that of a risk-neutral one. The output will be smaller, the larger its aversion to risk (Bigmann 1985).

According to Newbery and Stiglitz, the benefits of price stabilization include those benefits derived from the reduction of risk of price uncertainty, in addition to the transfer benefits—those derived from a change in the average income.

For producers, the risk benefits are determined by the degree of risk aversion and the extent of reduction in income or revenue variability; the revenue instability after stabilization is the output instability, assuming no change in supply conditions.

For consumers, the total benefit is equal to the sum of transfer benefits plus risk benefits and arbitrage benefits. The arbitrage benefits are pure social gains that the private storage activity is expected to capture, which remain unexploited because of market imperfections; they depend on the elasticity of demand and the variability of consumer prices. The risk benefits depend on the coefficient of risk aversion, the variability of consumer income and prices, and the correlation between consumer income and prices. For producers, high values of the coefficient of risk aversion and production variability can result in benefits. Similarly, for consumers, high values of risk aversion and high correlation between consumer income and prices can result in benefits to consumers. In such a formulation, the benefits depend on the variability of output, the coefficient of risk aversion, and the price elasticity of demand. The long-run effect of price instability depends on the response of supply to changes not only in mean price but also in its variability.

The Newbery and Stiglitz model also deals with the role of storage and draws attention to the dynamic aspects of price stabilization arising from that role; subsequent authors have extended the analysis of dynamic aspects considerably. The amount carried over in storage from one period to the next or the vacant storage capacity influences activities in the subsequent period. Thus, storage operations induce serial correlation in prices even if there is no such correlation in production because the price depends on the total quantity supplied during the year, including the quantity released from storage, which has accumulated in the previous year and is thus correlated with the previous year's price.

A number of studies have sought to elaborate on the incorporation of dynamic elements in price stabilization (Helmberger and Weaver 1977; Miranda and Helmberger 1988; Ghosh, Gilbert, and Hallet 1987; Wright and Williams 1991; Goletti 1992). Storage necessarily introduces a dynamic element into the market equilibrium through the size of the stocks carried forward, since in such a situation, prices and supplies in one year affect prices and consumption in the future. The expected price next year or in the next period depends on planned carryover to next year; the latter, in turn, depends on the expected prices this year or the period after. The amount of private storage depends on the extent of the price differential (change in price) between two points of time, that is, between the date of buying and that of selling. If the public authority attempts to change the magnitude of the price differential by undertaking public storage, it will affect the incentive for private storage, leading to an offsetting reduction in private storage.[2] Thus, in order to achieve a given price differential, the increase in public storage will have to be more than the amount of reduction in private storage. If the producers and consumers are risk neutral (that is, the cost of income risk is of no concern) and if the distribution of income between producers and consumers is not relevant, the optimum storage rule is the same as the amount that risk-neutral competitive private agents with rational expectations will hold. This is characterized by the condition that storage continues until price in the period plus storage cost per unit is driven to equality with the present discounted value of the future expected price. Under these circumstances, the optimum rule can be achieved by leaving the storage functions to the competitive market, provided that good forecasting services to ensure rational expectations are available as well as a full set of insurance markets to ensure risk neutrality.

If economic agents are not risk neutral and if one is concerned about distributing the benefits of stabilization through storage among producers and consumers, the optimum amount to be stored will differ from the amount required for competitive market equilibrium. Public intervention therefore is needed to increase social welfare; that is, combined consumer and producer surpluses must be properly weighted. Assuming that the social weight on producers exceeds that on consumers, the following conclusions emerge: with constant linear demand (inelastic over the relevant range), competitive storage and hence stabilization should be subsidized or supplemented; with constant elastic consumer demand, competitive storage and hence stabilization may need to be reduced if storage costs are high. In the latter case, the determination of the optimum degree of intervention depends on a comparison between the costs of further subsidization, on the one hand, and increased benefit from a reduction of producers' income risk plus an increase in transfers (weighted by the difference in consumer and producer weights), on the other (Newbery and Stiglitz 1981).

Therefore, whenever public interventions such as floor price or price-band schemes are considered, the interaction between private and public storage becomes an important variable in the analysis of the effects (costs and benefits) of such interventions. There are charac-

---

[2]Helmberger and Weaver (1977) showed that private storage is quite sensitive to demand and supply elasticities. The greater are the supply and demand elasticities, the smaller the difference between actual and expected prices. If stabilization programs are offset by private storage behavior, this may lead to more rather than less price stability. If private trade believes that expected prices in the next period will be greater than current prices plus storage costs, they would acquire stocks at the same time that the government is selling stocks. This would prevent the government from protecting ceiling prices, resulting in greater instability.

teristics of storage that make the analysis of the interaction between public and private storage critical. First, storage has an asymmetric effect on price. Without storage, the probability distribution of commodity prices is more or less symmetrical; with storage, it is skewed, the long tail being toward the high price. Second, although the agents who store do so in anticipation of shortages, they can store only when there is a surplus. Last, storers collectively cannot borrow from the future—storage cannot be negative. The ability of storage to work in one direction introduces nonlinearity into the system. If all of a carryover stock is consumed in a drought, it can be of no help if another drought follows immediately. The linkages that storage establishes between different time periods imply that storage in this period depends on the price that can be expected in the following period; yet the price in the following period depends on the aggregate storage in that period; the latter, in turn, depends on the aggregate amount stored in the more distant future. Therefore, current storage in part depends on the relationship between the amount in hand at some future date and the aggregate storage on that date.[3]

In the light of the foregoing analysis, the welfare implications of public interventions in storage introduce at least two complications. First, producers' benefits from storage are captured in land values with the result that producers who own land or commodities at the time of the intervention of the stabilization scheme benefit from changes in the value of wealth. The near-term boost to demand associated with an accumulation of stocks may be sufficient to raise producers' wealth, assuming they own land and that the commodity is available at the time of the introduction of the scheme. The initial boost occurs because the government must buy stocks before it sells and because the effect of any substantial resale is discounted. The public intervention that increases stocks may destabilize land values, even though it may stabilize prices. With no storage, price of land is constant, although the commodity price and producers' income vary. With storage, land values fluctuate inversely, varying in reference to movements in carryover.

Second, the benefits to producers in producer surplus, today and tomorrow combined, resulting from price stabilization, are different from what a comparative static analysis indicates. The estimation of current producers' surplus overestimates the expected gains (current plus future) for producers, since the carryover stocks depress prices and revenue in the future below what they would have been in the absence of stock. Similarly, the current consumer surplus underestimates the present value of the expected current surplus because what is stored will be consumed in the future and future consumer surplus should therefore be credited.

---

[3]The feedback of future storage behavior on current aggregate storage makes the task of solving for competitive equilibrium difficult, as it requires a stochastic dynamic programming exercise. It introduces a complex dynamic system that cannot be solved analytically for general solutions; it can only be solved numerically.

Thus the increase in rents in the current period may be less or more than the depressing effects on revenue in the future, caused by large carryover stocks involved in a price stabilization scheme. The conventional welfare analysis may therefore over- or underestimate the gain if intertemporal relationships, indicated above, are not incorporated.

The existence of a price floor may cause the average producer surplus over time to be lower than it otherwise would be. Although a floor price raises the minimum price, increased carryover reduces the chance of high prices in the future. As the scheme operates over many periods, accumulation proceeds and the carryover effect of stocks gains more weight.

Under a price-band scheme, the probable distribution of price, in contrast with no public intervention, is skewed so that ceiling prices are more likely to occur than floor prices. There can be no price below the floor price (so long as financing is not a limitation), but there may be prices above the ceiling because stocks may be inadequate to keep prices down, since they cannot be borrowed from the future. The price-band scheme imposes inflexible management of a public stock policy, with a tendency toward excessive stocks (Wright and Williams 1991).[4]

Deaton and Larouque (1992) introduce nonlinearity of commodity prices along with storage and draw implications for the price stabilization policy. In contrast with traditional approaches that assume linear price demand and supply functions, they emphasize the role of convexity (nonlinearity) in commodity prices. They argue that many basic foodgrains do not have substitutes; thus, the effect on the price of a shortfall in supply is likely to be larger, the smaller the supply. Since speculators are guided in their decision to hold inventory by expected future prices, the greater the convexity of the demand function, the more future supply uncertainty will increase future prices relative to current prices. The interactions of supply uncertainty, demand convexity, and the inability to borrow against future production are strong incentives to carry positive inventories. There will, however, be periods when current prices are so high that inventories will not be held; in those rare times when little or no stockholding is followed by large random shortfalls in production, prices will become extremely high. These price flare-ups would be difficult to explain without demand convexity and negative stocks.

Since negative storage is impossible and demand functions for commodities are strictly convex, the standard rational expectations competitive storage model predicts the existence of rare but violent explosions in prices, coupled with a high degree of autocorrelation in

---

[4]Miranda and Helmberger (1988) assume (1) private storage; (2) price-responsive production; (3) a price-band scheme, an exhaustible stock, and a predetermined support and release price; and (4) rational expectations. They show that only programs with a wider price band and lower supply price are able to stabilize prices without destabilizing revenue, in contrast to traditional models assuming that a price band always raises prices and stabilizes revenue. Also, they find that some price-band schemes that actually reduce the long-run market price below the competitive level and narrow the price band by lowering the release price may destabilize prices.

more normal times. Deaton and Larouque find that the long-run behavior of prices is probably not compatible with the linearity assumptions that characterize most of the models in the literature. Actual commodity prices are highly correlated, but the series displays occasional "flares" or "spikes" when dramatic increases are followed by equally dramatic decreases. Although these occasional flare-ups have implications for the success of price stabilization policy, the standard models that use linear demand functions cannot explain them.

Most of the analyses of price stabilization have concentrated on single market analysis: they look at price stabilization in isolated or single markets with no interaction with other commodity markets. But, most agricultural commodity markets are interconnected, and because of substitution between crops (in production and consumption), their prices are interrelated.[5]

In recent years, some researchers have used multimarket models (Braverman et al. 1992) as opposed to single market models to assess the consequences of price stabilization programs. They argue that the neglect of cross-market effects can lead to significant under- or over-estimation of the consequences for producer and consumer income. Price variability in a multimarket analysis depends on two additional factors: covariance of the error terms or disturbances affecting supply and demand functions and cross-price effects—how demand for one commodity is related to variations in the prices of the other commodities that are either complementary or substitutes. The effect of multimarket interaction on price instability is ambiguous. The higher the covariance of disturbance and the cross-price effects, the higher the price variability. Thus, if there is limited scope of substitution between crops, the cross-price effects will be small, as price instability in one market will not lead to price instability in another market.

The multimarket effects can be shown, assuming that there are no cross-price effects in the supply of the goods, but the model affects cross effects on the demand side. For simplicity, it is assumed that the goods are nontradable, so that world prices have no effect on the demand and supply of the two commodities, and there will be cross-price effects.

The demand (D) and supply (S) of wheat and rice, are written with subscripts, w and R, respectively.

---

[5]Income from a given crop is only one source of income variability; other crops or other noncrop sources of income exist. If a farmer is widely diversified and if income variability from one crop is not correlated with variability of income from other sources, it may not have a large effect on total income. If, on the other hand, variability of income from one crop is negatively related with other sources of income, the reduction of income variability for one crop will increase the overall risk. Moreover, since producers are concerned with real income, if prices of commodities purchased by them are positively correlated with the variability of income from the crop sold, then the variability of real income is less than the variability of many incomes. For consumers, the impact of price variability on the marginal utility of income is the crucial question. Unless consumers' income varies to offset price variability, real income is variable. Needless to say, consumers prefer stable to unstable consumption.

Solving each market separately, one obtains:

$$D_w = \alpha_w - \beta_w P_w + C_w P_R \text{, and} \tag{1}$$

$$S_w = \gamma_w + B_w P_w, \tag{2}$$

where D_w and S_w are demand and supply functions for wheat and P_w is the price of wheat.

$$P_w = \frac{\alpha_w + C_w P_R - \gamma_w}{B_w + \beta_w}, \tag{3}$$

$$D_R = \alpha_R - \beta_R P_R + C_R P_w, \tag{4}$$

$$S_R = \gamma_R + B_R P_R, \text{ and} \tag{5}$$

$$P_R = \frac{\alpha_R + C_R P_w - \gamma_R}{B_R + \beta_R}. \tag{6}$$

These equations show how multimarket effects can influence price instability. On the assumption that

$$\theta_w = \alpha_w - \gamma_w, \text{ and}$$

$$\theta_R = \alpha_R - \gamma_w,$$

the price instability equations for wheat and rice are derived by taking the variance of equations (5) and (6) as follows:

$$\sigma_{P_w}^2 = \frac{1}{(B_w + \beta_w)^2} \times [\sigma_{\theta_w}^2 + C_w^2 \sigma_{P_R}^2 + 2C_w \text{cov}(\theta_w, P_R)];$$

$$\sigma_{P_R}^2 = \frac{1}{(B_w + \beta_w)^2} \times [\sigma_{\theta_R}^2 + C_R^2 \sigma_{P_w}^2 + 2C_w \text{cov}(\theta_R, P_R)];$$

The effect of multimarket interaction on price instability is ambiguous. It depends on the covariance of disturbances in the supply and demand functions in one market and the price in another market, and the cross-price effects of the price of one commodity on the demand of the other commodity. The higher the covariance and the cross-price effects, the higher the price variability. Thus, if there is limited scope of substitution between crops, the cross-price effects will be small.

In a study in Brazil, Braverman et al. (1992) found that the quantitative effects of multimarket analysis do not differ significantly in producer and consumer benefits of price stabilization from a single market analysis. The study also finds that the risk benefits are smaller than the transfer benefits, as in the single market analysis. However, the multimarket analysis affects average outcomes significantly, such as the producers' or consumers' average income or surplus.

The impact on consumers' and producers' welfare has spawned a large literature over many years. This literature has grown in complexity as additional assumptions regarding the interaction between public and private storage, nonlinearity of supply and demand functions, and multi-community markets have been incorporated. The dynamic multiperiod analysis of the effects of price stabilization policies on welfare and market price provides results different from those yielded by comparative static analysis. As further progress is made in evaluating the microeconomic benefits of price stabilization at the analytical level, new insights can be expected. For example, the factors underlying the magnitude of risk aversion and their implications for the benefits to be derived from price stabilization require further analysis. Not enough is known about how a reduction in risk through greater price stability affects the efficiency of allocation of resources or choice of technique or supply response. Again, although findings to date indicating that risk aversion is low are consistent with the expected utility-maximizing behavior, they are not quite consistent with security-based theories of behavior in which the agent is primarily concerned with achieving a subsistence level of income and avoiding disaster (Newbery and Stiglitz 1981).

Poor, undernourished consumers in developing countries cannot decrease their food consumption when prices fall in order to save or store. In fact, when prices are high, they often must sell assets that are not easily replaced because they have saved little in good years. Instability has asymmetrical effects because the welfare impact of upward price movements is more negative than any likely positive impact from a downward price movement. That is why the popular outcry when food prices are increased is always louder than the praise when prices decline.

The poorest suffer the most when prices are high. In extreme cases, they die. Ravallion (1987) finds that short-run price instability caused an increase in mortality of a little under 10 percent during famines in Madras, India, and in Bangladesh. The increase in deaths due to price instability represented about one-third of famine mortality. Mortality risks are not accounted for in any of the welfare measures of price stabilization, obviously because of the difficulty in quantifying them. Even in less severe situations, analysis often neglects precommitted consumption—habits that make the consumer adverse to price instability (Kanbur 1984).

Macroeconomic and Economy-Wide Considerations

Besides the microeconomic benefits of price stabilization, there are macroeconomic effects—effects of food price changes that spill over to the rest of the economy. These macroeconomic aspects have so far not been explored in detail in the context of rigorous models in the same way that microeconomic aspects have been analyzed. The discussions so far have been mainly qualitative (Timmer 1989a; Kanbur 1984; Kanbur and Vines 1984; Newbery and Stiglitz 1981). Some of these studies have attempted to model a few macroeconomic aspects in an international context, but not in the context of a domestic economy. A rigorous analytical and quantitative treatment of macroeconomic aspects requires a general equilibrium framework, including an analysis of dynamic investment behavior.

To put the macroeconomic considerations simply, if the price elasticity of demand is low and the budget share of food is high, a given percentage change in expenditure leads to a large change in the absolute amount of expenditures relative to the rest of the economy. Thus, large changes in food prices are likely to lead to large changes in aggregate expenditures. Similarly, many cereal commodities traded in the world market fluctuate sharply. They are often positively correlated with domestic markets; in an open economy, price variations in the world market need to be absorbed through changes in food imports and foreign exchange budgets. This involves higher foreign exchange costs when prices are high and foreign exchange savings when world prices are low.

The effects of variation in foodgrain prices on the rest of the economy affect the risks faced by economic agents in other sectors. Prices in other sectors vary not only in response to their underlying demand and supply situation, but also in response to foodgrain price fluctuations. To the extent that risks in other sectors are increased, investment in other sectors is discouraged. This has significant consequences if investment is irreversible, which is the case with most investments in the real world (Pindyck 1988).

In the agriculture sector, it is easily seen that diversification of crops is a response to the price risk that farmers face. Diversification may, however, result in high-cost cropping patterns. Farmers have the option of specializing in one crop that suits their agroecological and managerial abilities or of producing several crops. They may choose to plant some crops that do not have a long run comparative cost advantage in order to spread the risk of fluctuations in supplies and prices. If farmers face stable prices, they are likely to specialize in the crop with the highest income. If, they face unstable prices (say, half of the time the price is high and half of the time the price is low), they will plant several crops in order to average out their incomes. That is, they will diversify their risks, even though the average expected income will be less than it would have been under the one-crop regime. Again, food price instability is accentuated by price instability in input markets. Increasingly, agricultural production in developing countries makes extensive use of modern inputs such as fertilizer, fuel, and high-yielding varieties of seeds. Hence, instability of prices and supplies of inputs that may be aggravated by inadequate stocks and the absence of insurance markets may induce output price instability. For example, if fertilizer becomes more expensive, farmers will plant less, output will decline, and the price of output will go up. Instability in fertilizer prices may lead to suboptimal levels of investment in domestic fertilizer production, which in turn may lead to increased dependence on world markets that are unstable.

If one widens the range of macroeconomic effects of food price instability beyond the agriculture sector, one can refer to the impact of price instability on inflation. When prices of primary commodities go up, there is pressure from urban workers for an increase in wages. Given that industrial wages are slow to adjust downward, declines in food prices are not followed by corresponding declines in wages and that triggers inflation (Kanbur 1984).

Apart from the upward push on prices over time, price instability may also cause the rate of inflation to vary. When a large share of the budget goes to foodgrains, the spillover effect of fluctuation in the foodgrain market on prices in other markets tends to cause variation in the overall rate of inflation. This is different from normal changes in prices due to changes in technology and preferences; a variable inflation rate, it has been argued, has a negative impact on investment and income growth (Timmer 1988; Dawe and Timmer 1991).

In developing countries, under conditions of uncertainty and imperfect capital markets, savings are used to buffer short-run fluctuations in income; such savings fluctuate as they are drawn down or added to in response to short-run changes in income. This implies that in poor countries such precautionary savings must be held in liquid form in order to be readily available in the short run. This discourages long-run investment (Deaton 1989). Stabilization of prices reduces the need for planning for contingencies at very low income levels thus enabling the rural population to focus on generation of savings. At the marketing level, instability in prices also leads to reduced investment in infrastructure and other public goods needed for the development of an efficient marketing system. A reduction in investment adversely affects economic growth (Dawe and Timmer 1991).

To the extent that price stabilization and reduction in uncertainty have macroeconomic and long-run investment-related benefits (Dawe and Timmer 1991), these benefits are provided simultaneously to all and therefore can be considered public goods. For example, the private sector is not likely to provide a socially optimum amount of storage. This makes a case for intervention by the public sector, since the social demand for stocks may exceed the effective private demand (Dawe and Timmer 1991).

Price stability also contributes indirectly to political stability. A sharp rise in food prices tends to cause unrest in urban areas where low-income food consumers are organized and vocal. Similarly, a significant fall in food prices may cause discontent among farmers and lead to rural violence. Price policies that avoid such sharp price fluctuations contribute to political stability and in turn have a positive impact on investors' expectations (Timmer 1988 and 1989a). In this context, it has been said that no government can "stand idle and watch people go hungry" because world prices have risen sharply, or watch farmers forced into bankruptcy or into urban unemployment because of a fall in prices, even if the government's actions may make the problem worse sometime in the future. Governments must be perceived to take action and intervene (Timmer 1988).

In conclusion, traditional micro welfare analysis to date has not made a strong case for foodgrain price stabilization, unless a large weight is attached to risk aversion, especially a strong desire to avoid the deprivation that high food prices impose on the poor at times of supply shortfalls. This seems broadly to be the case even when consumer and producer welfare is analyzed over time in a dynamic context by introducing such factors as the interaction between private and public storage, nonlinearity of demand and supply functions, and multicommodity markets. However, additional analysis is needed of risk aversion in the context of price stabilization. Also, as Kanbur (1984) points out, more work is needed to formulate and analyze decisionmaking in a way that produces results that do not appear contrary to the intuition that consumers dislike price instability. In the meantime, macroeconomic considerations such as low inflation, high and stable investment, and overall economic and political stability linked to food price stability require further rigorous examination. And, Newbery and Stiglitz (1981), who say that the benefits of price stabilization have been overestimated by other writers, stress that it is the quantified microeconomic benefits (based on the analysis to date) that are overestimated, not the total benefits.

4

Some Operational
Aspects of Food
Price Stabilization
Policies

While the foregoing chapter dealt with the "why" of food price stabilization in developing countries, this chapter highlights a few operational aspects of price stabilization—the "how" of price stabilization. Although the governments' objective was to stabilize real prices, they operated by influencing nominal prices. That is, a public agency intervened in the market to influence or determine nominal prices, but in the periodic revision of nominal support prices or ceiling prices, they took account of the prices of other relevant input and output prices. To analyze the operational aspects of price stabilization, it is necessary to distinguish between the two major types of instability. The first arises between two harvest periods in the same crop or calendar year and is called seasonal (or intrayear) instability. The second arises between years and is called interyear instability. Interyear instability is unpredictable in the long run in the sense that one does not know, for example, when a severe drought will occur. On the other hand, the direction if not the size of short-run seasonal variation is predictable, since prices are likely to be low during harvesting season and will rise during the lean season of the year.

Stabilization of prices encompasses both inter- and intra-annual price variations. In fact, these two types of instability are interrelated. If instability is aggravated from one year to the next, seasonal variations will increase. Depending on whether the year is good or bad, the size of the harvested crop will be larger or smaller than in the same season of the previous year. In a price stabilization policy, interventions necessarily take place in given seasons. The target price in a given season around which variations are permitted is determined with reference to an annual target price. Therefore, the floor and ceiling of seasonal variations in a price stabilization scheme are usually built around the floor and ceiling of annual variations. It is not possible to implement, for example, a band around an annual target price without having a band around seasonal price variations (Ahmed 1988).

A second important consideration associated with any stabilization scheme is the type of market structure, that is, whether the market is oligopolistic or competitive and whether markets are spatially integrated or not. Segmentation of markets implies that a segment of the market with excess demand does not get any feedback from other markets that have excess supply. In this case, the transmission of prices among markets is absent. In general, markets are neither totally segmented nor totally integrated. Empirical evidence has shown that markets in developing countries are often not fully integrated (Ravallion 1987; Ahmed and Bernard 1989).

The most commonly used stabilization schemes in developing countries are a buffer stock policy or a combination of buffer stock and trade policies. Production in a given period equals the change in stocks plus net exports plus consumption. If prices are not to respond fully to production variations, they need to be offset by variations in trade or stocks rather than by variations in consumption. Therefore, the degree of price fluctuation—the margins within which prices are allowed to fluctuate—is closely related to either stock changes or changes in trade (Pinckney 1986, 1988, and 1989; Bigman 1982).

The basic idea behind the buffer stock policy is that when there is excess production and producers receive low prices, the government buys grain and stores it for the next period. Consequently, the demand schedule for that commodity shifts to the right so that the price producers receive (and consumers pay) goes up. In the next period, the government sells the stocks. That effectively shifts the supply schedule to the left, so that the commodity is traded at a lower price. The objective is to maintain levels of stocks such that fluctuation of the commodity's price between periods falls within the desired limits. Frequent fluctuations in production shorten the length of time during which stocks need to be held.

The rationale and the incentive for holding stocks is much stronger in the seasonal case: if output is harvested in the first quarter, for example, then in the next three quarters, consumption requirements have to be met either from stocks or from imports. In view of the lag between planning orders for imports and the actual arrival of a shipment of imports—at least a full quarter in many developing countries—having stocks to release in the rest of the year is essential. In view of the short time interval, imports cannot always substitute for stocks. But this seasonal pattern in food production does not necessarily provide an argument for public stocks; private stocks may be adequate to achieve a reasonable degree of price stability.

As stated above, a stabilization scheme with public intervention in storage and marketing usually has to define a target price around which stabilization is sought. There are several rules. First, there is the world price rule under which the target price is the one prevailing in the world market. The second rule is the domestic cost rule. The basic principle of domestic cost pricing is the "full average cost;" frequently, the support or lower-band floor price for a crop is set at a level covering its unit cost of production. Another rule for price fixation is the income parity rule, which seeks to attain a predetermined ratio between the incomes of rural and urban workers (Scandizzo, Hazell, and Anderson 1984).

The effect of a buffer stock on price stability depends on how the trigger price—the price at which the buffer stock is sought or sold—is determined. The trigger price is based either on a fixed-band rule or on an adaptive-band rule, around an estimated mean price. An adaptive band around the target price incorporates the effects of the supply response, since it is based on the moving average of past price movements. The fixed-band rule disregards the behavioral response of producers to a reduction in price fluctuations. If government attempts to stabilize the price around a mean level, failing to take into account the supply response resulting from the reduction in price instability and consequently in risk, it faces a steady accumulation of stocks and thus suffers increasing losses.[6] These losses will force the government to stabilize prices at a lower level. If farmers cannot foresee the future policies of the government, they cannot predict the government's equilibrium price. If farmers believe that a public authority will continue to determine the price, as it did before, whereas it actually adjusts its policy to take account of the supply response, then farmers will be expecting a higher price than the one that will ultimately prevail. This misconception could lead to an overallocation of resources and welfare losses.

Price stability can also be achieved by varying imports and exports. When, for example, a domestic commodity is scarce due to adverse weather conditions, the government can import this commodity and hence prevent the price from rising. However, one basic requirement for such a policy is that the markets be integrated, so that when trade takes place, the commodity will be distributed equally among regions (that is, the supply schedule of all regions will shift to the right). This policy differs from buffer stocks in terms of geographical or spatial distribution. Buffer stocks can be held in several regions, whereas imports have to be brought to a port of entry, from which point distribution to buyers in different regions is handled by private distributors. This means that buffer stocks may not require as high a degree of market integration as trade.

High transaction costs in trade lower the cost of storage relative to the cost of trade. The cost of foreign trade includes the costs involved in making trade inquiries, collecting and processing trade intelligence, making contacts with buyers or sellers, and negotiating purchases and prices. It also includes charges for transportation, bagging and handling of exports, and the excess costs of handling exports beyond the costs incurred for handling domestic foodgrains. The operation of buffer stocks is effective when the commodity is nontradable or the government controls imports and exports. In the absence of constraints or restrictions on foreign trade, it will be profitable for traders to buy from

---

[6]Serial correlations in production can reduce the effectiveness of buffer stocks. In the presence of serial correlations, bad years are followed by bad years; if it is so, the storage facility will remain empty or full (in a series of good years) and thus idle for longer periods of time. As a result, the overall effective price stability is smaller as storage activities are fewer; also more capital is locked in and results in high interest and operation costs. An adaptive rule in this context can increase the effectiveness of stocks in reducing price instability.

the stock and export when international prices are above the levels at which the buffer stock would sell, a step that would quickly deplete the stocks. The converse is also true when the world price falls below the stock's buying price; the incentive is to import the product and sell it to the stockholding agency, a step that will deplete the country's financial resources.

So far as the role of trade in compensating for changes in domestic production and in stabilizing prices is concerned, a distinction needs to be drawn between countries that are regular importers or exporters and those that are nearly self-sufficient, with a surplus in some years and a deficit in others. The habitual or regular exporter or importer can more easily and successfully rely on trade adjustment, varying exports or imports, as the case may be, to moderate the impact of fluctuations in domestic production on prices. The reliance on trade as an efficient means of stabilization is enhanced if the commodity concerned is widely traded and readily available in the world market.

In a country that is an irregular or occasional exporter or importer, the domestic market clearing price is frequently below the import parity price and above the export parity price. This is partly because the country has no established trade connections or channels in world markets for the particular grain. Not being a regular international trader often indicates that the quality of the crop is not competitive and does not meet international standards. Also, the internal cost of transportation, marketing, and distribution from and to the export and import points may be high. The gap between import and export parity prices may be so high that the country may find that holding stocks as price differentials more than compensates for domestic storage costs. A country that exports at a very low price may suffer losses because it is likely to pay high prices for imports when needed to supplement domestic production.

An appropriate combination of reliance on trade and on domestic stocks will depend on the costs of exporting and importing, the world price of the foodgrain in question (and corresponding export and import parity prices), domestic storage costs, and the desired degree of price stability. The case for holding domestic stocks is stronger, the higher the domestic production variability, the higher the transaction costs for engaging in foreign trade, the greater the preference for domestic staples, and the lower the price elasticity of demand.

For meeting interyear fluctuations, Pinckney (1989) suggests that reliance on foreign trade is preferable to public stock policy because of the high cost of buffer stocks, whereas buffer stocks are more appropriate for stabilizing seasonal price fluctuations. This does not necessarily imply, however, that reliance should be placed on public stocks to the point of discouraging stocking activities of private traders. Since seasonal price movements are predictable, not random, and occur because it costs money to store grain from one season to another, they can be dealt with through the stock operations of the private sector, including private engagement in the export and import trade, so long as the price differentials between seasons cover costs.

A policy of reliance on trade to stabilize prices can be combined with a variable tax and subsidy policy. The rates of taxes and subsidies on imports and exports can be changed in response to variations in world prices to keep domestic prices within the desired degree of variation. If the tax rate is progressive, it tends to smooth out the impact of variations in the world price on the domestic price. When the world price rises, the higher marginal tax rate on exports, if the foodgrain is an export commodity, prevents the domestic price from increasing proportionally. Import taxes work in the opposite direction. A scheme of taxes and subsidies can be combined with the operation of a buffer fund if taxes and subsidies involved in the price stabilization policy are not to be merged with the operations of the general budget. When the price is high, the commodity is taxed, and the tax proceeds accumulate in the fund. On the contrary, when the price is low, the commodity is subsidized and resources in the fund are drawn upon.

It has been argued that if the objective of the government is to protect consumers from upward price variability, then an effective alternative policy is to provide rations at a fixed but lower than normal price. To be cost effective, rations should be extended to a large section of the population; at the same time, the amount of foodgrain to be supplied as rations should be modest, keeping the cost of food distribution low (Newbery 1989). Targeted rations are more cost effective than universal rations. However, targeting particular groups like small farmers or industrial workers is not likely to cover all the poor. Thus, issues remain on how effective is the coverage or how socially costly is limitation on the coverage. Identifying the target groups and delivering food rations to them without leakages is not easy. The cost of administration of such a scheme is often very high. However, when rations are costly or the ration system cannot be extended to a large section of the population, stabilization of prices through public or private storage may be a preferred alternative. If the government undertakes additional storage above the competitive equilibrium storage (where the market price includes the storage, interest, and transportation costs), it will be beneficial for the consumers who do not store, even if producers are compensated for the resulting price falls due to storage. Additional storage results in a market price lower than would otherwise prevail when shortages in the market occur; hence, income is transferred from producers to consumers. If producers are not compensated, consumers will derive additional benefits. Storage can be financed by a progressive tax on foodgrain consumption, with consumers paying a tax in accordance with their food consumption.[7]

---

[7]If consumers have access to unbiased future markets (one in which the future price is an unbiased estimator of the future cash price) and have perfect information, they would be able to choose a better hedge. Even in this scenario, additional storage by the government would be desirable for consumers, so long as storage is more expensive for consumers than for larger commercial traders (Newbery 1989).

Costs of Price Stabilization

The direct costs of price stabilization include interest costs of the financial capital required to purchase and sell food stocks, transport and handling charges, rent of physical storage facilities, and any wastage of food stocks that may occur in storage as well as the cost of management and organization of the agency. To the extent that the margin between selling and buying prices is not adequate to cover costs, then subsidies need to be paid; similarly, there is a need for subsidy if there are losses in external trade.

The margin between the buying and the selling price must cover the direct costs of stabilization mentioned earlier, if the stabilization agency is not to suffer losses. If the agency is able to enforce a price regime in the market through its buying and selling operations, which do not cover costs, private storage will be discouraged; only those efficient private traders who are able to function at low margins will remain engaged in private storage. Thus, if the price spread implemented by buffer stock operations is extremely narrow, fewer supplies will serve the market and thus might end up aggravating price instability. As private traders are displaced, if the narrow price spread (unattractive to private traders) is implemented by government storage operations, the government will increasingly need to take over the storage function (Newbery and Stiglitz 1981; Pinckney 1989). Subsidies to private traders will be needed to provide incentives if private traders are to be induced to stay in business.[8]

Moreover, if traders and farmers expect that the government agency is unable to enforce the price at the announced level, they will speculate by postponing selling or unloading their stocks to make larger profits. If only a small number of producers provide marketable surplus, and only a few traders are engaged in trade, this small group can create considerable instability in the market price. Stability in a government's policy is crucial in determining the expectations of traders and farmers.

---

[8]Assume that interest plus storage costs are equal to 10 percent of the value of the amount stored and that the average amount on storage is equal to 20 percent of the annual crop. Without government intervention, the price will be 10 percent greater at $(t+1)$ date than at (t) date. If demand elasticity is e, the quantity supplied in the market at (t) is $(0.1e)$ greater than at $(t+1)$. As assumed above, 20 percent of the crop is stored with the producers. Now, assume that the public agency wishes to reduce the price difference between (t) and $(t+1)$ from 10 percent to 5 percent, and that it seeks to do so by buying $0.025e$ of the amount supplied at (t) period and keeping it until $(t+1)$. Thus, the amount consumed between (t) and $(t+1)$ would be $0.05e$ rather than $0.1e$, because the amount consumed at (t) goes down by $0.025e$ and goes up at $(t+1)$ by $0.025e$. Thus, price variation declines by half. However, if the price rise in $(t+1)$ falls below 10 percent, there will be no private stockholding and all private stockholders will dump their holdings (about 20 percent of the total supply) in the market. To prevent the price from falling, the agency will have to bring it up so that it purchases $(0.025e + 2)Q$ (Q being total quantity supplied); this implies that with the demand elasticity, $e = 0.5$, the amount bought and stored by the agency would be 17 times larger (Newbery and Stiglitz 1981).

If there are dual markets for foodgrains—if, for example, the government sells foodgrains at prices lower than open market prices and if prices in the government outlets are stickier than in the open markets—the public agency will confront large swings in demand as consumers move back and forth between public and private outlets. This increases the amount of stock the public authorities need to hold because they have to deal with these swings as well as with harvest fluctuations.

Under certain circumstances, the opportunity costs of public storage may be low. Because of fragmented credit markets, for example, the government agency may procure credit at a lower interest cost than the private traders can obtain. This is because the government agency has a higher credit standing, since the size of the government's assets allows the agency to bear risks more easily. Moreover, it has been argued that efficient storage, which depends on the use of fairly well-defined technology in a minimum number of locations, is the kind of activity that the government is least likely to bungle. This activity is unlike that of processing and quickly transporting grain from a large number of individual producers and selling it to consumers dispersed throughout the country. This type of activity—processing, transporting, and retailing—requires considerable micro information about the needs and preferences of individuals or groups of producers and consumers, and the government does not usually perform this activity efficiently or well. Whether the advantages of cheap credit and large-scale storage are more than offset by the inefficiencies of mismanagement due to improper profit incentives depends on the particular circumstances of a government (Dawe and Timmer 1991).

The indirect or external costs of price stabilization incurred or imposed outside the foodgrain sector mainly arise from the possibility that financing of stabilization programs destabilizes either the government budget or the availability of credit in the rest of the economy. Moreover, in an open economy, varying exports or imports in an attempt to stabilize prices may cause variations in the foreign exchange budget of the government or in the private exchange market. A policy of stabilizing prices through buffer stocks requires funds for procuring and distributing food stocks in order to effect the supply of food in the market. In other words, the price stabilization agency has financial needs that fluctuate from year to year and season to season, which in turn destabilize the resources available for government expenditure. This is because the amount of food that needs to be procured and distributed to defend the floor and ceiling prices cannot be accurately predicted in advance. The impact of such unpredictable variations in government expenditure on other sectors of the economy can be offset by the provision of a separate fund for price stabilization, which is independent of the rest of the budget; this fund can be drawn on in a year of good harvests and replenished in a year of bad harvests. This fund provides the agency with considerable flexibility to respond at short notice to its operational needs, instead of having to negotiate financing every time it requires resources. Management of the contingency fund must be strictly disciplined:

temporary surpluses in the fund must not be spent for purposes other than price stabilization.

There are other ways to finance buffer stock operations. The stabilization agency can have a flexible credit line at the central bank to draw on as needed. However, this may destabilize the money supply and affect price movements in the rest of the economy. But any destabilizing effect on the overall monetary balance can be offset by the central bank. The central bank can vary the aggregate money supply to accommodate changes in credit needs of the buffer stock operations by taking into account the impact of the buffer stock operations on the overall money supply. Therefore, any instability generated in the rest of the economy due to the operations of buffer stocks can be dissipated or compensated for by appropriate monetary policy or a contingency fund with independently allocated resources.

In a net food-importing country, where fluctuations in food prices arise partly because of fluctuations in world food prices, the stabilization agency would need to vary its expenditure on foreign exchange resources depending on (1) the extent of the changes in domestic food production, and (2) the degree of fluctuation in world prices. Where foreign exchange is allocated under a system of exchange control, foreign exchange resources available in the rest of the economy will be destabilized; alternatively, where the exchange rate floats freely, it may fluctuate in response to the varying demand on foreign exchange for food imports, with destabilizing effects on the rest of the economy. However, in both instances, the spillover effects on the rest of the economy can be offset by providing foreign exchange resources that are specifically earmarked for food imports; the variations in expenditures on food imports would be met by variations in the fund of foreign exchange resources, especially earmarked for buffer stock operations.

If the government's implicit objective is to transfer income between income groups, aside from price stabilization per se, another component of indirect costs is involved. This is incurred by maintaining an "average" stabilized price, which is different from the "average" nonstabilized price. The difference in these two average prices times the quantity traded equals the income transferred. In this case, estimating the true cost of stabilization requires a different approach because the government would have incurred costs anyway to implement the objective of income redistribution. This is an important issue because, to assess the costs of price stabilization correctly, they should be distinguished from the costs involved in efforts to distribute income or consumption, so that selection of the appropriate stabilization scheme can be made without being burdened by additional objectives.

5

Alternatives to Price Stabilization: Crop Insurance and Futures Markets

Crop insurance can be an efficient way of spreading the risk among farmers and regions, across sectors of the economy, and, most important, over time. In practice, however, crop insurance has been disappointing, especially in developing countries. Insurance on agricultural commodities in developing countries is rarely offered, mainly because its cost is high. While the normal administrative costs for, say, life insurance are between 1.0 and 1.5 percent of the value of the total coverage, for crop insurance these costs may be as high as 6 percent (Hazell, Pomareda, and Valdés 1986). This is attributed to the large number of small farmers, the wide diversity of crops and agricultural practices, and a lack of trained personnel. Therefore, insurance policies from private companies are not available. Even when crop insurance is heavily subsidized, many lower-risk farmers—those with good managerial skills—are not willing to purchase contracts on a voluntary basis. Only high-risk farmers, with low managerial competence, are likely to purchase insurance, thus requiring the government to charge higher premium rates.

An insurable risk has three characteristics. First, the probability that the event will occur must be readily quantifiable. Second, the damage it causes must be easy to evaluate. Third, the occurrence of the event or the damage it causes should not be affected by the insured's behavior (absence of moral hazard). For example, crop damage due to pest attack is not insurable; the likelihood that it will occur is hard to quantify; its actual occurrence and the damage caused are often difficult to verify, particularly when there are other causes of crop loss; and the farmer, through negligence, can increase the likelihood of occurrence and the amount of damage incurred. Most market risks, such as fluctuations in prices of outputs and inputs, and resource risks, such as interruptions in supplies of inputs, labor, or credit, and production risks, such as pests, diseases, excess humidity, and excessive temperature changes, are not strictly insurable (Hazell 1992).

Crop insurance usually compensates a farmer for yield losses caused by a wide range of hazards. Compensation is usually calculated as the difference between normal and actual yields valued at the compensation price. The insured causes of yield loss are so comprehensive that in practice it is almost impossible to exclude damage from uninsured causes when assessing losses. Such insurance is often provided by public-sector insurance agencies and often heavily subsidized by the government; private insurers avoid it. Many insured risks occur so frequently that premiums are too high for most farmers to afford. However, these policies seldom insure losses due to a fall in output prices. Yield-based compensation helps protect against a fall in income when price does not rise with a fall in output. Price fluctuations often cannot be separated from fluctuations in demand and in yield. Moreover, price fluctuations themselves affect demand and supply so that a change in price multiplied by normal output or output prior to the price change does not indicate a net loss in income.

The absence of insurance markets is also due to the problems of adverse selection and moral hazard that exist in agricultural markets (Stiglitz 1987). Frequently, the farmer knows the hazards he faces better than the insurer. For example, it is unlikely that the insurer knows the exact differences between the types of soil found on a farm. A farmer can only insure the crop that is grown on low-quality soil, which has a high probability of failure and hence a high probability of receiving payment from the insurance company. This is adverse selection. Also, the farmer may be tempted to reduce costs, thus increasing the probability of crop failure. For example, the farmer can apply less fertilizer, less water, or even less labor, reducing the cost of production but increasing the probability of failure. This is moral hazard. These are hidden actions that the insurance company cannot observe.

Another reason for the lack of insurance in agricultural markets is that crop failure is a global problem in the sense that a flood, drought, or other natural disaster affects all the farmers of a particular region or country, so that the losses to be compensated become too large. This is called a covariability problem. An insurer can only survive economically if the insurance scheme spans a large number of farmers or regions with negative or positive but weakly correlated variations in income, prices, or risks. In addition, the costs of administering insurance for a large number of small farmers spread out over a wide region are high.

Even in developed countries such as the United States, private crop insurance programs have not been successful. Among the reasons cited for this failure are (1) inadequate coverage of prices as well as yield risk; (2) inadequate geographical dispersion; (3) insufficient data for a sound actuarial program; and (4) improper timing and wide variety of contract sales leading to adverse selection problems. After the private sector made several unsuccessful attempts in the early 1900s, the U.S. government became involved. The crop insurance schemes undertaken are really a kind of subsidy, but they tend to subsidize the farmers that engage in activities with high probabilities of moral hazard and adverse selection, rather than farmers who need a subsidy (Stiglitz 1987).

Another alternative for reducing uncertainty about future revenues caused by price fluctuations without reducing price variability itself is use of futures markets. This can be done, for example, by hedging, that is, by selling forward at a price determined on the date on which the contract is made, but with payment to be made on delivery. Similarly, for commodities for which there are organized futures markets, farmers may sell futures in the commodity and close out the transaction by buying back futures corresponding to the delivery month when production will be sold. If the price of the crop goes down, the futures contract can be covered at a lower price. If the price goes up, the farmer will be able to sell the futures at a higher price, thus breaking even. Forward and futures prices move in line with cash prices; hence, selling forward does not reduce price variability, but it reduces uncertainty regarding revenues.

A farmer who is risk averse will plant more of a "safe" crop, one for which the price is certain, and less of a risky crop, one for which the price is higher but variable. When a farmer fully hedges by selling a risky crop forward, the relevant comparison is between the forward price of a risky crop and the expected price of the safe crop; price fluctuations are no longer relevant. However, a risky crop will still be at a disadvantage because forward prices will represent the "risk component" and the forward price is quoted on the basis of an expected price discounted by a risk factor. The "certainty" equivalent of the uncertain future price is less than the mean of the likely range of prices that may prevail in the future.

Futures markets do not eliminate production risks. Once the contract has been signed, the farmer is obligated to sell even if he does not produce; in other words, the farmer has to pay the difference between the futures price and the spot price prevailing on the maturity date. Although futures markets are primarily designed to reduce a part of producers' risks arising from price variability, other traders enter the market with the objective of maximizing profits. These speculators are likely to have considerably more information regarding the future movement of prices than farmers do. The farmers are at a disadvantage and, therefore, the futures market becomes unattractive (Stiglitz 1987). Moreover, futures markets have short time horizons. While they are adequate for short-run allocation of inputs, they do not offer any flexibility in investment in the long run where price uncertainty becomes a major impediment. Even in developed countries, few farmers resort to futures markets to meet their price risks, probably because transaction costs are too high and because small farmers suffer from a lack of market information relative to large traders and may be afraid of market manipulation (Timmer 1989a).

Small farmers in developing countries do not have access to organized futures or forward markets. They probably can reap the benefits through a marketing intermediary or traders or marketing boards. The latter can contract with farmers for forward delivery and offset the risk that prices will be higher by delivery time by selling an appropriate quantity of futures on the exchanges that serve world markets. At the time of planting, the marketing board announces the price at which it is committed to purchase a commodity at the harvest date. This price is based on the current price quotations for the month when the board will take delivery of the quantities it purchases from farmers. The board then sells futures corresponding to the delivery month to offset its risk position with the intention of selling the futures at the time it takes delivery of the commodity and sells it to its normal customers. The problem is how to ensure that farmers will comply with forward contracts between themselves and the board. If, at harvest time, spot prices are higher than the contracted futures prices, farmers will have an incentive to renege and sell to the market.

Floor price guarantees are a variant of forward-pricing schemes; they maintain farmers' willingness to participate, thus reducing enforcement problems. A forward-price contract eliminates or substantially reduces the price risk faced by farmers and allows them to estimate the profitability of alternative courses of action. By contrast, a floor price guarantee eliminates the worst risks but provides a generally low return. With a suitable price guarantee, farmers can plan without worrying that they are jeopardizing their financial viability.

The marketing agency, in this case, offsets its risk position by purchasing an appropriate number of "exchange put" options, conferring the right to sell the commodity at a future time. Farmers will exercise the option only if prices fall below the floor. The agency can finance the operation through a general tax on exports of the commodity (if it is an export commodity). The cost of offering a price guarantee that is significantly below the future postharvest price at the time of planting is likely to be small. If the crop is an import commodity and there is no futures market in it, the government faces a problem in providing the guarantee of a floor price. In this case, there is no suitable instrument that the government can use to offset its risk position. No commodity exchange finds it profitable to provide a contract; any available instrument, in view of transport costs or grade differences, provides only poor hedges for the price risk involved. In this case, the alternative could be an import tax when the import price falls below the guaranteed floor.

Where there are no easily implementable alternatives for offsetting the risks and uncertainty caused by food price instability, price stabilization schemes augmented by buffer stocks or trade measures continue to be the stabilization methods of choice in many developing countries. Lack of experience with use of futures markets in the domestic foodgrain markets in developing countries and unsatisfactory experiments with insurance schemes in a few countries contribute to this. It should be noted that the alternatives to price stabilization emphasized in this chapter deal with producers' risk and not consumers'. The interest of consumers is often served by public distribution of staple foodgrains, especially to low-income consumers.

6

Price Stabilization
Policy: Rationale
and Objectives

The first part of this review looked at the macro and micro considerations that underlie the attempts by governments in developing countries to stabilize prices by intervening in the foodgrain
market. It also examined alternative policies that do not seek to stabilize
prices as such, but deal with the consequences of the risks that price
instability generates for food producers and consumers. The next four
chapters consider the price stabilization experiences of five Asian countries. Chapter 6 discusses the particular circumstances underlying price
stabilization policy in each country. Chapter 7 reviews in detail the
design and implementation of the price stabilization measures adopted
in each country to derive lessons that may be relevant for similarly
situated countries in Asia and elsewhere. Chapter 8 assesses the impact
of price instability policy over time and across countries, and Chapter 9
provides a few quantitative estimates of the benefits of price stabilization
policy.

The countries selected for study take diverse approaches to inter-
linked price objectives and instruments used for price stabilization. All
the countries focused on the one or two cereals (usually rice and wheat)
that are most important in their consumption basket and the production structure. In one case the basic cereal was important both in the
domestic consumption basket and as a foreign exchange earner. In
another case a cereal crop was more important as an export crop than
for domestic consumption. In all cases but one, the major cereal crop
was an import-substituting commodity; hence, price stabilization policy
was an important component of an overall policy to reach a higher level
of self-sufficiency. All of the countries achieved a considerable degree of
import substitution through a combination of price and nonprice policies. Several countries generated export surpluses in some years and
were either marginal or substantial importers in other years.

In all five countries, the cereal sector occupies a major place in the
production structure and as a source of rural income; food is a large
proportion of aggregate household expenditure, especially for the poor.

In the Philippines, crops accounted for 58 percent of the total value
added of the agriculture sector in 1990. Paddy rice accounted for
29 percent and corn for about 12 percent, a dominant share in agricultural production. In Indonesia, as late as 1990, rice constituted 29
percent of the agricultural value added (World Bank 1992). In Bangladesh, in 1989–90, cereals (rice and wheat) constituted 75 percent of total

crop production. In the late 1980s, rice constituted 54 percent of the agricultural value added and 35 percent of the total income of all rural households. In Pakistan, food crops accounted for more than 50 percent of the total agricultural value added as late as 1990; the shares of wheat and rice in total agricultural value added were 29 and 13 percent, respectively. In Thailand, rice constituted 30 percent of exports as well as of the total agricultural value added. Rice farmers constituted 35 percent of the total population, 65 percent of the agricultural population, 50 percent of the total rural population, and 66 percent of the rural poor.

In all five countries, cereals had a major share of the consumption basket of the poor. Between 20 and 22 percent of the total expenditure of the poor in the Philippines was on rice, and between 6 and 10 percent was on corn. The urban poor spent 18 to 21 percent of total expenditure on rice and 2 to 5 percent on corn. Overall, the poor spent 25 to 30 percent of their total expenditure on rice and corn combined (Balisacan, Clarette, and Cortez 1992). As late as 1980, 60 to 80 percent of the total energy intake of poor households in both rural and urban areas of Indonesia was derived from rice (Sudaryanto, Hermanto, and Pasandran 1992). During the 1980s, rural households spent between 61 and 75 percent of their total income on food, while urban households spent 39 to 62 percent. Calories per capita per year from kilograms of rice were 150 kilograms compared with 56 kilograms from other cereal and nonfood crops. In late 1990, 88 percent of the total average per capita calorie intake of the rural poor in Bangladesh and 83 percent for the urban poor were derived from rice and wheat. In Pakistan, during the 1970s, more than 60 percent of the poor's income was spent on food; by 1984 that share had decreased to 53 percent (Pakistan, Ministry of Food, Agriculture, and Cooperatives 1988). By the mid-1980s, more than 56 percent of the food expenditure of the poor was on wheat and rice; the share of wheat and rice in total food expenditures of the poor ranged between 17 percent in urban areas and 30 percent in rural areas in the mid-1980s. This, in effect, amounted to 9 to 13 percent of the aggregate per capita expenditure of the poor (Naqvi and Burney 1992). At the same time, in Thailand, the share of grains and cereals (predominantly rice) in the total expenditures of rural and urban poor households ranged from 25 to 30 percent in 1975 and 16 to 22 percent in the late 1980s (Siamwalla et al. 1992). Given the relative importance of cereals in the income of farm households as well as in average food consumption baskets, instability in cereal prices is a serious matter.

Price Stabilization and Related Objectives

All countries sought to moderate price fluctuations from one season to another and from year to year. However, this objective was pursued in the context of a number of interrelated objectives, ensuring a floor or an incentive price to producers and a ceiling price to consumers in order to protect them, especially the urban consumers, from a high or sudden rise in food prices. In most countries, there was some kind of public distribution of the cereal commodity to designated consumers, with varying degrees of coverage. The price policy objectives for output must be seen against the background of an overall policy of increased food self-sufficiency pursued by Asian countries through increased investment and a variety of price incentives, including input subsidies. At the same time, the indirect effects of the macroeconomic and trade and foreign-exchange regimes discriminated against agriculture. The cumulative result of these policies, both short- and long-run, in the majority of the countries was a divergence of domestic foodgrain prices from world prices.

In the Philippines, the provision of income support to producers and affordable prices to consumers was a principal objective of price policy. In practice, the policy was intended to prevent or smooth out sudden movements in food prices away from prevailing prices in response to changes either in world prices or domestic supplies. Supplying rice to consumers at a stable and reasonable price was considered politically important. In the public perception, changes in government such as in 1961 and 1965 were associated with high prices and a shortage of rice (Intal and Power 1990). With the memory of the political consequences of high food prices in the 1960s fresh, failure to provide rice at a reasonable price was tantamount to failure to solve the country's food problems; it tended to erode the government's credibility and legitimacy. Also, low and stable rice prices were considered important for keeping the rate of inflation low, reducing upward pressure on wages, and improving the profitability of the industrial sector. There was less concern about the price of corn, since it was only consumed by a small fraction of the population. Until the 1960s public policy regarding corn focused on white corn, which was not internationally traded. Imports of yellow corn increased sharply, however, with an increase in hog and poultry production. Import substitution through increased domestic production of corn and high levels of protection became an important policy objective. This policy favored producers over consumers: producers were poor corn farmers, while consumers of chicken and pork were largely high-income urban dwellers. The variability in the domestic price of corn was to be moderated by varying the rates of protection for domestic production.

In Indonesia, Pakistan, and Bangladesh, the stabilization of food prices was linked to the objectives of ensuring low, stable prices for predominantly urban consumers and protecting farmers from price fluctuations, both seasonal and annual. In all three countries, public distribution of food to designated consumers was a high priority. In Indonesia, for example, the national food stabilization agency, Badan Urusan Logistic (BULOG) was responsible for providing monthly rice rations to a "budget group" (military and civil-service personnel). BULOG also ensured emergency food supplies for relief in earthquakes, floods, and droughts (through government relief centers or village leaders and local marketing channels) when private trade was disrupted. The on objectives changed over time in Indonesia. In the early years, distribution of rice to the budget group was assigned top priority, followed by prevention of an abnormal rise in urban rice prices and defense of the floor price of rice for farmers. During that period, the provision of rice rations to the budget group was considered politically important for ensuring the loyalty and efficiency of the civil service and military. By the late 1970s and 1980s, the civil service and the military were no longer heavily dependent on rice rations to maintain their real incomes; therefore, the pressure to keep monthly rice distribution as a top priority was reduced. Food rations became a way of providing salaries in-kind (rather than in cash) and were valued by BULOG on the basis of cost plus profit.

In Bangladesh and Pakistan, the most important objective was to provide food at an affordable price to designated consumers. The system of public urban food distribution covered all classes of the population, irrespective of income groups, but it covered only major urban centers. Coverage in the rural areas was limited to the very poor, and actual distribution was limited because supplies were inadequate and leakages were considerable. In addition, in both countries, the public distribution system covered most civilian and military employees. In 1990/91, for example, public distribution in Bangladesh, which accounted for 13 percent of all foodgrain consumed in the country, covered industrial workers, all government employees, and low-income rural households. It also included distribution of food through food-for-work and feeding programs for vulnerable groups such as poor women and children (Ahmed 1992).

In all three countries, there was a great push toward self-sufficiency in food as early as the 1960s in Pakistan and in the 1970s and 1980s in Indonesia and Bangladesh. The goal of self-sufficiency in rice was accorded high priority in the government's investment and price policy in Indonesia. Support of the floor price of rice was considered a necessary incentive for adoption and wide diffusion of new agricultural technology such as high-yielding and disease- and pest-resistant varieties of rice. Bangladesh and Pakistan stressed the importance of assuring farmers of an incentive price at harvest time as an encouragement for expanding the use of modern inputs. In Pakistan, emphasis was on self-sufficiency in wheat and in Bangladesh it was on rice. Pakistan had not achieved its objective as late as the 1980s; significant quantities of wheat were imported during that decade. There was a major debate in Bangladesh during the 1970s about the relative merits of output price support and input subsidy as instruments for stimulating agricultural growth. But an input subsidy—on fertilizer, for example—did not prevent the collapse of postharvest prices. Hence, output price support policy and fertilizer subsidies were considered complementary rather than substitutes. Essentially, the support price announced in advance was expected to stimulate the use of yield-enhancing input by reducing uncertainty, rather than by raising the expected value of returns (UNDP 1988). Only in 1977 was stability of prices introduced as an objective of Bangladesh's food distribution system. Policy was designed to moderate the rise in the food price in the lean season through open market sales by the government foodgrain agency. This was unrelated to the objectives of guaranteeing an incentive price for farmers and a low and affordable price to designated consumers at all times.

Similarly, Thailand's objective was also to assure low, stable prices for a designated category of consumers. At first, the primary emphasis was on provision of food at low prices to civil servants, whose salaries in the post-World War II period were eroded by inflation. A cheap rice price policy was a substitute for salary increases and was treated as a way of forestalling demand for higher wages. Later, when the urban working class grew in the wake of industrialization, the promise of stable, low food prices to urban labor classes became an important objective. Providing a support price for the farmers was not an important objective until the 1970s when it emerged as a political concern, though not a significant one (Panayotou 1989b; Siamwalla et al. 1992). All throughout, however, the objective of maximizing foreign exchange earnings from rice exports by maintaining a high, stable export price retained high priority. Rice price policy in Pakistan took a similar path. The objective in stabilizing the rice price was different from that for stabilizing wheat, because rice was not a principal cereal in the food consumption basket in Pakistan. The objective was to maximize foreign exchange earnings and to earn high profits for the Pakistan Rice Export Corporation by driving a wedge between the export price and the farmer's price.

A review of past objectives in the different countries, therefore, indicates that price stabilization per se, in the sense of reducing the variability of prices by a certain percentage, was not the sole objective. Retail prices paid by designated consumers and the prices received by producers were of greater concern as the countries embarked on policies to accelerate domestic food production.

7

Design and Implementation of Stabilization Policy

How the public sector or the government intervenes in the foodgrain market to stabilize prices is shown in Figure 1, which depicts the interrelations among the different components and functions of the domestic marketing system. The main interactions are among public procurement, sales and distribution, public stocks, and foreign trade (exports and imports, including food aid). The marketing system receives supplies through private trade with farmers, as shown by the arrow proceeding upward from production, from own stocks (not shown in the figure), and from open market sales from public stocks by the public agency. Consumption is met directly from farmers' own production, from private supplies of the marketing system and from public distribution of public stocks. Public stocks are built up through public procurement from farmers and traders or from imports; public stocks and food aid jointly fill the coffers of the public distribution system. Exports can come from private traders in the marketing system and public stocks; imports can also be brought in by either a public agency or private traders. The participation of private traders in export and import trade was not allowed in most countries until the late 1980s or early 1990s.

Fluctuations that occur in domestic food production must be offset by fluctuations in consumption or in public or private stocks, in foreign trade, or a combination of the three. A fall in output, for example, will cause the price to rise, unless consumption falls correspondingly, or stocks are released, or imports increase, or exports fall, or any combination of these possibilities.

As was seen in earlier chapters, public stocks are the main instrument for implementing price stabilization policy. Public stocks are operated with the help of (1) domestic procurement and (2) imports in the case of import-substituting commodities. Export crops, such as rice in Pakistan and Thailand rely on the regulation of the quantity of exports through public monopoly or through a system of variable taxation of exports undertaken by private traders.

The relative importance of imports and domestic procurement varies over time and across countries, depending on the stage of self-sufficiency that a particular country has reached. The higher the import

Figure 1—Flow chart of a stylized foodgrain market

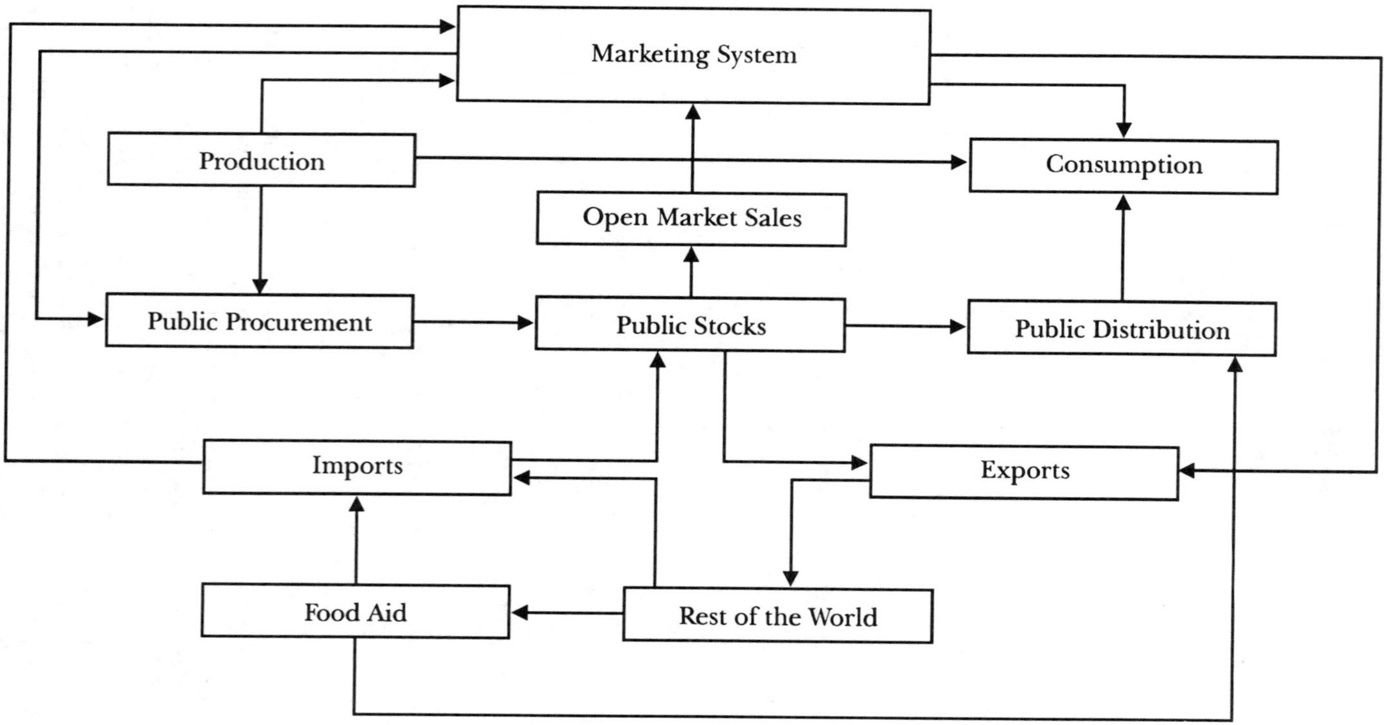

dependence of a country, the greater is the role of variations in volume and prices of imports in determination of domestic price variability. As a country reaches self-sufficiency, fluctuations in domestic production assume a dominant role in determining the variability of food supplies and prices, especially when foreign trade is restricted or regulated.

In order to analyze the implementation of price stabilization policies, one must distinguish between the food-importing countries and the food-exporting countries. Food-importing countries have similar objectives as well as similarities in design and implementation of stabilization policies different from those pursued by the exporting countries. Stabilization policies in Bangladesh, Indonesia, Pakistan, and the Philippines focus on import-competing cereals: wheat or rice as the case may be. The instruments used for implementation of these policies are the use of public stocks and imports through a system of open market sales, public distribution, domestic procurement, and imports by a public agency.

Price Stabilization Policies in Importing Countries

Stabilizing Role of Imports

External trade in rice and wheat was monopolized by the governments of Bangladesh, Indonesia, Pakistan, and the Philippines. In Pakistan the government abolished its monopoly in rice in 1988/89; in Bangladesh, the rice monopoly in external trade did not end until 1992/93. Rice exports in Thailand were always in the private sector. Although the quantity of food imports was regulated to offset fluctuations in domestic production, the balancing operation was seldom very efficient. In Bangladesh and Pakistan, imports were based on a forecast of domestic demand, estimated on the basis of population and assumed rate of per capita grain consumption, and production. The gap between domestic consumption and production represented import requirements. Whether these import requirements could be met depended on food aid and the availability of foreign exchange for commercial imports. How much food aid would be available from one year to the next was uncertain. There was no multiyear commitment of food aid to indicate the total amount of food aid that would be available in years to come, thus allowing annual allocation or utilization of food to be determined in response to changes in import requirements from year to year. The availability of food aid each year was subject to annual negotiation with the donor. Given the food aid available, the amount of commercial imports to be financed from a country's own foreign exchange resources was determined by the aggregate availability of foreign exchange resources, on the one hand, and competing demands for their use, on the other. In the allocation of foreign exchange resources to food imports, however, the requirements of public food distribution received high priority. Most imports were distributed through the public food distribution system rather than through private trade. If there was a shortfall in production, it was expected that public food distribution requirements would increase, and imports would have to be larger as a result. Because import requirements varied not so much in response to price changes as to food aid availability and requirements of the public distribution system, there was no direct relationship between the quantity of food imported and variations in domestic food prices. However, since the amount of food distributed by the system was determined by the estimated food production and since future price movements were related to the expected variations in supply, including changes in production and stocks, food imports were indirectly related to expected price changes (Goletti 1993).

In the Philippines, on the other hand, the public distribution system was not a major channel for stabilization operations. Imports were sold in the open market. Therefore, even though import targets were not rigidly related to expected movements in prices, the quantity of imports to be undertaken by the government was influenced by price movements to a much greater degree than in Bangladesh or Pakistan. There was also more flexibility in Indonesia, where imports varied directly in response to price changes because of a comfortable foreign exchange situation, especially following the oil boom of the 1970s and 1980s.

In the Philippines, large rice imports helped keep prices stable during 1963–67 and 1971–77. So long as the country was a net importer, and the domestic price of rice was in excess of the border price because of import restrictions, a rise in the border price could be absorbed by relaxing restrictions and reducing the scarcity margin on imports, thus preventing the transmission of an increase in the border price to the domestic market.

When border prices rose sharply in the Philippines either because of a rise in world prices or because of an exchange rate devaluation, the domestic price of rice (especially the retail price) was not allowed to rise as much as the border price. Price control, antihoarding, and other measures were undertaken in order to keep the rice price low. During 1971, when there was a shortage of rice, imports were not significantly expanded to prevent a rise in the domestic price. This was done partly to maintain the domestic price at a level that would provide the desired incentive for increased domestic production; moreover, during this period foreign exchange resources were too scarce to finance an adequate increase in food imports.

In Indonesia, during the period 1960–80, imports' role as a balancing wheel for stabilizing prices was considered essential. Imports enabled the price stabilization agency to be flexible about the total amount of rice that was released, especially during 1977–80, when rice imports to Indonesia were 20 percent of the total world trade in rice. Until 1984, Indonesia was a net importer of rice. After that, domestic procurement generally assumed a more important role than imports as an instrument for achieving price stabilization, although there were occasional years, such as 1987 and 1991, when imports played a crucial role in stabilizing prices. Similarly, in 1985 and 1986 rice was exported to defend the floor price. Even when imports were not a significant proportion of domestic supply, they were an expeditious means of supplying urban areas. It was easier to obtain supplies of rice from urban ports and to inject them into retail markets than to obtain supplies from domestic procurement that provided administrative and logistic problems for the food agency. Also, imported rice was of higher quality than domestically procured rice—a factor of some importance in urban areas. During the 1970s, on the one hand, rice imports were subsidized when the world price was higher than the domestic ceiling price to the benefit of consumers in urban areas where these imports were primarily distributed. On the other hand, imported rice was taxed when the domestic price was higher than the world price in 1984. Temporary surpluses exported in 1985 and 1986 were subsidized since the world price was lower.

Since the mid-1980s, Indonesia has become more self-sufficient in rice and the relative importance of imports as a source of supply has declined; pressure not to rely on imports for meeting short-term dips in domestic output has been strong. There was a political compulsion to establish the claim that the country had reached self-sufficiency; any attempt to import, even in years of shortage, was seen as reneging on this claim during the 1980s. Accordingly, an attempt was made to rely exclusively on domestic stock to maintain price stability. BULOG's operations became more complicated with the shift of the source of supply from imports to domestic procurement; local warehouses and mills and the transportation network had to be reoriented so that supplies from far-flung production centers could be moved to the centers where consumption, both urban and rural, was high. Imports only came into the country at a few points. From these, supplies could be distributed to major centers. This was easier than the task of procuring rice and transporting it from many regions and centers to major points of collection and processing for distribution and sales at wholesale and retail levels.

Relative Importance of Imports

The average share of imports in five-year averages in the net supply of cereals in the various countries is shown for three different cereals in Table 1. However, shares varied from year to year, sometimes greatly. For example, although the share of wheat imports in net supply in Pakistan declined over time, imports varied widely from year to year, which helped to balance out the fluctuations in domestic production. On the basis of annual shares, the highest and lowest shares of wheat were as high as 24.0 percent and as low as 0.2 percent during the 1960s, 18.4 and 3.1 percent during the 1970s, and 13.0 and 2.6 percent during the 1980s (Pakistan 1992). On the basis of five-year averages, the import share fluctuated between 12 and 19 percent during the 1960s, between 8 and 12 percent during the 1970s, and between 4 and 9 percent during the 1980s.

In Bangladesh, as well, variation in wheat imports was the principal means of compensating for fluctuations in domestic production; wheat

Table 1—Cereal imports as a percentage of net supply

Country/	Five-Year Average		
Commodity	1960s	1970s	1980s
		(percent)	
Bangladesh			
Rice	n.a.	2.9 to 1.9	2.0 to 1.9
Wheat	n.a.	87.4 to 63.8	57.3 to 64.8
Pakistan			
Wheat	18.5 to 11.7	11.5 to 8.4	3.8 to 9.1
Rice	10.7 to 6.3	18.0 to 31.3	31.1 to 34.2
Thailand			
Rice	−19.6 to −13.3	−11.0 to −16.0	−24.0 to −32.0
Philippines			
Rice	9.5 to (−0.5)	9.0 to (−3.0)	− 4.5 to 3.3
Corn	1.1	3.5 to 3.7	2.4 to 8.7
Indonesia			
Rice	n.a.	6.6 to 8.2	3.6 to (−1.0)

Sources: Balisacan, Clarette, and Cortez 1992; Bangladesh Bureau of Statistics 1991; Chowdhury and Shahabuddin 1992; Pakistan, Finance Division 1992; Siamwalla et al. 1992; and Sudaryanto, Hermanto, and Pasandran 1992.

Notes: Negative numbers (those with minus signs) indicate exports. All others are imports. The numbers in parentheses indicate a change from imports to exports in certain years.

This table gives the lowest and highest five-year averages (not individual years) for each of the three decades. n.a. is "not available."

was much more important than rice as a balancing factor in the total supply of foodgrains. The five-year average share of imports in the net supply of rice varied from 2.9 percent to 1.9 percent during the 1970s and from 2.0 percent to 1.9 percent during the 1980s. Over a five-year average, the share of wheat imports in net supply ranged from 87.4 percent to 63.8 percent during the 1970s and 57.3 percent to 64.8 percent during the 1980s. Counting the year-to-year variations in the share of imports, the highest and lowest shares of rice were 5.0 percent and 0.4 percent during the 1970s, and 4.5 percent and 0.4 percent during the 1980s. The highest and lowest shares for wheat were 96 percent and 69 percent during the 1970s, and 69 percent and 51 percent during the 1980s (Chowdhury and Shahabuddin 1992).

In the Philippines, the share of rice in net supply was smaller than that of wheat in Pakistan but higher than that of rice in Bangladesh. Moreover, the share of rice in net supply varied much more in the Philippines than it did for Pakistan's wheat imports or Bangladesh's rice imports—the two principal cereals consumed in those countries. During the 1960s and 1970s, rice production fluctuated to such an extent that the Philippines was a net importer in some years and a net exporter in others. For example, the five-year average share of rice imports or exports in net supply varied between imports as high as 9.0 percent of net supply and exports at 3.0 percent of net supply during the 1970s. Similarly, during the 1980s, the five-year share of exports varied between −4.5 percent of net supply and imports of 3.3 percent of net supply. On an annual basis shares varied between 12 percent as imports and 6 percent as exports during the 1970s, and from 10 percent as exports in some years to 10 percent as imports in other years (Balisacan 1992). The highest and lowest shares of annual imports of corn in net supply were 0.1 percent and 7.7 percent during the 1970s, and 0.6 percent and 14.5 percent during the 1980s (Balisacan 1992). On the basis of five-year averages of exports and imports, the range of fluctuation was narrower, ranging from 3.5 to 3.7 percent during the 1970s and 2.4 to 8.7 percent during the 1980s. For both rice and corn, exports and imports played an important role in stabilizing supplies.

In Indonesia, the share of rice imports in net supply was higher than that in Bangladesh but less than that in Pakistan; five-year averages varied from 6.6 to 8.2 percent during the 1970s and from 3.6 percent of imports to exports of 1.0 percent during the 1980s. On an annual basis, the highest and lowest shares of imports in net supply in individual years were 11.0 percent and 4.2 percent during the 1970s and 8.6 percent and 0.11 percent during the 1980s. However, there were years when rice was exported in order to dispose of surplus domestic production: exports constituted 1.3 percent and 0.6 percent of net supply in two successive years in the 1980s (Sadaryanto 1992).

For export crops such as rice in Pakistan and Thailand, the share of exports in net supply was much larger than the share of imports in total supply in other countries. For example, in Pakistan, the share of exports in net supply of rice went up over the years, ranging from five-year averages of 18 to 31 percent during the 1970s and from 31 to 34 percent during the 1980s. In Thailand, the share of exports in net supply, while going up over time, varied from a five-year average of 11 to 16 percent during the 1970s to 24 to 32 percent during the 1980s.

In all countries, variations in imports were used to offset fluctuations in domestic procurement. The years in which domestic procurement was large, imports were small and vice versa. In Pakistan, domestic procurement and imports varied in inverse relation to each other. However, imports were not always fine-tuned to offset production variations partly because there were errors in forecasting import requirements and partly because there were delays in import arrivals. In Bangladesh, where rice imports were not an important proportion of the total net supply, variations in wheat imports were used to offset changes in domestic production of total foodgrains (both rice and wheat). Since the release of foodgrains by the government agencies in Bangladesh and Pakistan was tied to the requirements of the public distribution systems, rather than to any specific price target, the variations in imports to offset variations in domestic procurement were therefore more closely tied to the public distribution requirements. In Indonesia, however, variations in imports to offset domestic procurement were more closely tied to variations in price. To some extent, this was also true in the Philippines. However, implementation in the Philippines suffered from shortcomings in the sense that the arrival of imports did not always coincide with seasonal variations in domestic marketing.

There were, in fact, two problems in regulating imports relative to fluctuations in domestic production and also relative to the public distribution requirements in countries such as Bangladesh and Pakistan. First was bureaucratic rigidity—delays and inefficiencies in implementing the import program. There were considerable leads and lags in adjusting import flows to variations in domestic production or expected movements in price. This was less so in Indonesia where BULOG, the stabilization agency, had more autonomy and flexibility in its operations. Second, there was the problem of forecasting errors in estimating import requirements. In the Philippines, forecasting was estimated to be off by 10 percent during the 1970s and 1980s.

In Bangladesh, forecasting errors were sometimes compounded by a political compulsion to overstate food shortages and import requirements. In view of the political risks attached to an abnormal rise in prices, the government often erred on the side of overestimating shortages. This was more likely in the case of floods than of droughts. Damages to crops caused by floods were often compensated for by subsequent crops in the next season: failure to take this into account led to overestimation of damages. The burden of excessive imports following natural calamities was aggravated by the buildup of farmers' stocks as output recovered in the next season. This was partly because the government's memories of the abnormal rise in food prices that led to famine in 1972–73 and its disastrous political consequences for the government of the day never faded away. Moreover, because food imports were monopolized by the public agency, there were possibilities for the agency to obtain large rents from imports, which could be appropriated by both politicians and bureaucrats.

Procurement, Magnitude, and Efficiency of Management of Domestic Stocks

Domestic procurement and distribution by the public agency was the most important instrument for stabilizing prices for import-competing cereals. Procurement and distribution were used to alleviate seasonal instability, whereas imports were used to deal with year-to-year fluctuations.

Purchases by public agencies were mainly intended to provide a price floor for wholesalers or farmers. The average ratio of procurement to domestic production of rice during five-year periods from the early 1970s to the late 1980s ranged from 7.6 to 0.6 percent in the Philippines, from 2.9 to 7.4 percent in Indonesia, and from 1.3 to 3.4 percent in Bangladesh (Table 2). In Pakistan, however, the ratio of procurement to domestic production for wheat was much higher. It varied between 12.7 and 31.1 percent during the period.

In the 1960s and early 1970s, the National Food Authority in the Philippines procured less than 2 percent of the total crop production. At that time, the Authority's main source of supply was imports. As domestic production increased, the National Food Authority increased its paddy procurement as a means of defending the paddy support price. The ratio of procurement to production increased from the mid-1970s onward. The range of variation in this period was 4 to 10 percent (Table 3). However, in the late 1980s, the ratio of procure-

51

Table 2—Average ratio of procurement to production, 1961–65 to 1986–90

(percent)

Period	Philippines Rice	Indonesia Rice	Pakistan Rice	Bangladesh Rice	Philippines Corn	Pakistan Wheat	Bangladesh Wheat
1961–65	n.a.	n.a.	n.a.	n.a.	n.a.	0.5	n.a.
1966–70	2.9	n.a.	n.a.	n.a.	n.a.	11.9	n.a.
1971–75	0.6	2.9	20.3	1.5	n.a.	12.7	n.a.
1976–80	7.6	4.1	32.5	3.4	n.a.	21.4	12.1
1981–85	6.1	7.4	35.6	1.3	2.2	26.2	8.8
1986–90	4.3	5.7	34.5	2.7	2.2	31.1	7.7

Sources: Balisacan, Clarete, and Cortez 1992; Bangladesh Bureau of Statistics 1991; Chowdhury and Shahabuddin 1992; Pakistan, Finance Division 1992; Siamwalla et al. 1992; and Sudaryanto, Hermanto, and Pasandran 1992.

Note: n.a. is "not available."

Table 3—Highest and lowest ratios of public procurement to production

(percent)

Period	Philippines Rice	Thailand Rice	Indonesia Rice	Pakistan Rice	Bangladesh Rice	Philippines Corn	Pakistan Wheat	Bangladesh Wheat
1961–65	n.a.	n.a.	n.a.	n.a.	n.a.	n.a.	0.0–1.9	n.a.
1966–70	0.9–5.1	n.a.	n.a.	n.a.	n.a.	n.a.	0.2–15.5	n.a.
1971–75	0.0–2.1	1.0–2.0	1.2–4.5	6.1–28.5	0.1–3.2	n.a.	2.8–17.6	n.a.
1976–80	4.1–10.1	7.0–12.0	1.9–7.9	23.9–37.6	1.8–6.0	n.a.	10.9–25.8	1.2–16.0
1981–85	2.4–9.3	n.a.	4.2–10.4	31.9–40.3	0.9–2.1	0.4–3.8	18.2–35.2	1.3–14.7
1986–90	2.2–6.7	n.a.	4.4–9.1	25.8–41.3	0.9–5.2	0.0–6.3	24.2–41.9	4.7–8.3

Sources: Balisacan, Clarete, and Cortez 1992; Bangladesh Bureau of Statistics 1991; Chowdhury and Shahabuddin 1992; Pakistan, Finance Division 1992; Siamwalla et al. 1992; and Sudaryanto, Hermanto, and Pasandran 1992.

Note: n.a. is "not available."

ment to production on average was lower than in the late 1970s. For example, even though production increased consistently throughout the 1980s, the average level of annual procurement declined by 20 percent between the first and second half of the decade, mainly because of financial stringency.

The ratio of procurement to production varied greatly from year to year, but did not bear a close relationship to the changes in production from one year to another. This variation was more a function of the financial resources that the National Food Authority could obtain in annual appropriations from the Ministry of Finance. The Authority was assigned a volume target for procurement. Given the uncertainty of crop production, however, it was impossible to determine the amount of grain that should be procured ahead of time. During 1985–89, when production increased, the procurement ratio in fact fell. However, the impact of increased production on domestic prices in a given year could be cushioned by exports as well as by procurement. For example, during the 1980s, the total procurement of paddy as a percentage of total production was higher in years when the Philippines was a net exporter than in years when it was a net importer. During 1980–83, when the Philippines was a net exporter, the percentage of procurement averaged between 6.2 and 9.3 percent, whereas it was 5.0 percent in 1984 and 2.4 percent in 1985—years when the country was a net importer. At that time the size of domestic procurement moved in tandem with the size of the imports and not necessarily with the size of domestic production.

The timing of procurement was not always fine-tuned to have the maximum impact on price instability. During the 1970s the largest procurement by the National Food Authority frequently occurred one or two months after the harvest peak. This can be explained by delays in remittance of funds from the central office to the regional offices. The consequences were serious; only those farmers who harvested late or had the capacity to store for one or two months were able to sell to the government. Thus, procurement tended to benefit the financially well-off farmers who had storage capacity. Moreover, inadequate intervention in defense of the floor price implied that the opportunities to sell at the official floor price were rationed. There were quality restrictions on paddy that was purchased by the National Food Authority. Rice of poor quality was to be accepted at a lower price, but it was often refused entirely. Farmers often found it difficult to get cash payments for their sales; the Food Authority often paid with checks that could only be cashed at certain banks. Farmers were obliged to hold passbooks issued by the provincial offices of the National Food Authority, which were intended to ensure that only legally recognized operators or owners of rice farms were able to sell to the National Food Authority at a fixed amount per hectare. Rice in excess of this amount or rice produced by tenants who were not legally recognized could not be sold to the government agency. The passbook requirement discouraged sales to the National Food Authority (Unnevehr 1985).

The National Food Authority had to secure its funds and sources of credit every year with prior approval by the legislature. If paddy prices were driven down because of a bumper crop and the National Food Authority had already exhausted its limited funds, private traders entered the market at prices that had no relation to the price target set by the government. In fact, over the years, the National Food Authority seldom reached its annual quantitative targets for procurement. On the whole, it reached no more than 70 percent of its target.

In the early years in Indonesia, procurement operations suffered from some of the shortcomings evident in the Philippines, such as limited availability of financial resources and procurement targets that were fixed quantities rather than relative to seasonal and annual variations in price. The limited financial resources created incentives on the part of the marketing agency to buy as cheaply as possible. These shortcomings were particularly evident during the 1960s. In principle, however, the job of the marketing agency was to support farm prices by procuring unlimited quantities at floor prices and none at all if prices were higher than the floor rice. In practice, in order to obtain rice as cheaply as possible, the purchasing agents often conspired with the rice millers and traders in surplus areas to drive down the market price. In fact, when sufficient quantities were purchased for public distribution to the budget group, procurement operations were terminated, even if prices plunged (Arifin 1992). During the 1960s, BULOG's operations were hampered not only by inadequate and inflexible resources, but also by a shortage of trained personnel to undertake its marketing operations. However, as Indonesia gained experience in procurement operations, measures were adopted to provide BULOG with adequate resources. It was during the late 1970s and 1980s that defense of the floor price received top priority as a way of stimulating domestic rice production.

During 1974–78 market prices were high due to persistent problems of shortfalls in production caused by pests and diseases. Under the circumstances, defending the floor price was relatively easy. In subsequent years as high-yielding plant varieties that were resistant to pests and diseases became available, the stage was set for a surge in food production. Defense of the floor price with an adequate incentive for profitable farming was crucial for the wide adoption of this new technology.

The share of procurement in production during the entire period 1970–90 ranged from 1.2 to 10.4 percent in Indonesia; the share was consistently higher in the 1980s than in the 1970s, but average rice production was also significantly greater in the later period. Not only was there an increase in the average quantity procured during the 1980s, but there was also an increase in the ratio of procurement to output during that period. However, year-to-year variation in the amount procured or in the ratio of procurement to output did not follow the annual variations in production closely. Imports, stocks, and price movements at the farmers' level all affected the volume or the ratio of procurement to output. BULOG procured rice paddy from farmers' cooperatives as well as from private traders. The role of the farmers' cooperatives (called KUDES) as a source of supply for BULOG grew over time; in some years, the proportion obtained from the cooperatives was as high as 90 percent.

The story was much the same in Pakistan. Until the mid-1960s, the share of wheat procured by the government was rather insignificant. The government purchased wheat directly from the farmers at harvest time in competition with the private traders. During the period 1967–76, the proportion ranged from 12 to 17 percent; the proportion of output procured by the government increased between 1976 and 1990, ranging from 25 to 41 percent. The absolute amount as well as the proportion of output of wheat procured, in general, went up, as the production of output of wheat over time went up. However, the variations in the absolute amount or the proportion of procurement from year to year were not always in close consonance with the absolute amount of year-to-year fluctuation in production.

The procurement target of the public agency in Bangladesh was determined on the basis of such factors as the requirements of the public distribution system and stocks in public storage. On average, prior to 1975/76, when stocks were low to start with, domestic procurement and imports rose together from year to year. From 1976 onward, as sizable stocks were built up, imports and domestic procurement were inversely related in an attempt to maintain stocks at the desired level, mostly to meet the needs of the public distribution system. In 10 out of 15 years, production increased and the ratio of procurement to production went up as well. However, the procurement ratio was not regulated in a systematic way with a price target in view. Between 1975/76 and 1989/90, the ratio of procurement to output was less than 2 percent in six years. Every time there was a severe shortfall in rice production, as during the years 1974/75, 1979/80, and 1986/87, the ratio of procurement went up—sometimes significantly—in the following year when production increased. For example, the ratio of procurement to production of rice went up to 3.2 percent in 1975/76 and to 6 percent in 1980/81; again, following very low procurement in 1986/87, the ratio of procurement to production rose in three successive years from 1.9 percent in 1987/88 to 5.2 percent in 1989/90 (Goletti 1993; Chowdhury and Shahabuddin 1992). In the case of wheat, the ratio of procurement to output was considerably higher than that for rice, reaching as high as 10 percent in 6 out of 14 years, and as high as 16 percent in one year. This was mainly because the largest percentage of domestic wheat supply was channeled through the public distribution system. Even though the ratio of procurement to output went up as aggregate output increased, there was no fine-tuning of the ratio of procurement to output in response to variations in production.

A number of factors reduced the effectiveness of the procurement operations in implementing price support in Bangladesh, such as an inadequate number of procurement centers; cumbersome payment procedures, which raised transaction costs for small farmers; lack of adequate financial resources; and, finally, collusion between traders and officials, which enabled traders to capture the margins between the market price and the procurement price (World Bank 1990). Excessive imports, particularly in good harvest years, frequently used up effective storage capacity, resulting in abandonment of the domestic procurement programs in the middle of the harvesting season. Procurement was mostly undertaken from farmers cum traders. The share of procurement directly from farmers was small, about 2 percent for wheat and 3 percent for paddy (Osmani and Quasem 1990). In 1988 the government started procuring from the rice millers on the basis of a fixed commission related to the procurement price. The millers, however, purchased paddy from the farmers at the prevailing market price and sold rice to the government at the procurement price, which was usually higher. Also, from the late 1980s onward, procurement was more flexibly related to the objective of price support as well as to the need for open market sales in lean months. The amount of procurement was thus constrained not so much by any quantity target but by the availability of funds and storage capacity.

To sum up, the Philippines and Indonesia were the two countries that had procurement policies that were related to price targets rather than to quantity targets. However, in the Philippines, the flexibility of open market policies or procurement was constrained by rigidity in access to finances, even though the National Food Authority was expected to buy when market prices fell below supply or floor prices. The food required for distribution to budget groups also created some rigidity in Indonesia.

During the 1980s, Indonesia had a higher ratio of procurement to output of rice than did the Philippines and Bangladesh. Pakistan and Bangladesh had quantity targets for procurement, heavily dominated by the requirements of a public distribution system that did not vary much from year to year, even though withdrawals or releases from the public distribution system were partly influenced by the difference between the market and "ration" prices. Much of the food distribution through public feeding programs and food-for-work projects, especially in Bangladesh, was governed by other criteria, such as the objective of long-term alleviation of poverty. In view of the multiple objectives of the public food distribution system, which relied partly on domestic procurement, it was not possible to distinguish the amount of procurement that would have been required to stabilize prices.

The procurement-to-output ratios also differed substantially between Bangladesh and Pakistan. The case of wheat in Pakistan was comparable to that of rice in Bangladesh because both are important food staples. In Bangladesh, wheat was also a staple, though secondary to rice, which was an export commodity in Pakistan. The ratio of procurement to output of wheat in Pakistan was consistently several times higher than the ratio of procurement to output of rice in Bangladesh. This was because the public distribution system in Pakistan was much larger and was supplied mainly by domestic procurement.

Public Distribution and Open Market Sales

While the procurement of foodgrains by the public agency was designed to influence the lower bound or floor price in a price stabilization policy, the sale of foodgrains either in the market or through direct public distribution was intended to influence the upper bound or ceiling price. The countries differed widely in their systems of public distribution or sale of foodgrains in the market. In the Philippines, there was no public food distribution directed to designated consumers. In Indonesia, food was both distributed to designated consumers and sold in the open market. Bangladesh and Pakistan relied mainly on the public distribution system for designated consumers. In the Philippines and Indonesia, sales from government stocks were intended to moderate rises in price and were geared to price movements in the retail markets. When the retail price of rice rose above the release or ceiling price in the Philippines, the government sold rice in the open market from its own stocks. Traditionally, the National Food Authority intended to cater to the low-income groups. With this end in view, the major part of its supplies for sales in the open market were obtained from imports and were of low quality; the price ceilings were fixed based on ordinary variety of rice for low-income groups.[9] During the 1980s, the ratio of public distribution of rice to total consumption of rice ranged from 6.2 percent in 1980 to 11.2 percent in 1990 (Philippines, Department of Agriculture, 1990). There was an increase in the ratio of public distribution to total consumption of rice. In some years—1984 and 1990, for example—in response to a rise in the retail price, the National Food Authority increased the ratio of public distribution to total consumption of rice. The average ratio was on the whole higher than the average ratio of procurement to total output, except during the period 1976–80.

In Indonesia, the percentage of total consumption of rice covered by public distribution was about 12 percent during the late 1970s, declining to 8 to 9 percent during the 1980s. In fact, the percentage of consumption covered by public distribution was slightly higher than the proportion of production that was procured by the price stabilization agency. However, there were two channels of public distribution of rice in Indonesia. One was intended for the budget group (the civil and military officials and the state enterprise employees). This amounted on average to a distribution of 1.7 million metric tons[10] of rice a year.

The second channel was open market sales undertaken in response to variations in the market price vis-à-vis the ceiling price. Open market sales were intended to moderate rises in the market price and to keep it within bounds, preferably below the ceiling price. But the share of open market sales in total public distribution in Indonesia declined over time. During the late 1970s, open market sales, as a proportion of public distribution, were 60 percent or more;

---

[9]The National Food Authority not only engaged directly in open market sales and purchases, but also regulated wholesale, processing, milling, and warehousing activities. It operated and owned more than 300 warehouses and more than 200 procurement stations, many of which also provided additional storage. The National Food Authority, in addition, owned rice mills in the grain-growing areas.

BULOG in Indonesia had a total storage capacity of about 3.5 million tons with 1,434 storage warehouses. It employed about 7,000 people in its operations across Indonesia (Ellis 1993a).

[10]In this report, all tons are metric tons.

in the 1980s, the highest percentage ever reached by open market sales was about 30 percent, and that was in one year only (World Bank 1990; Umali 1985). Throughout the period the amount distributed to the budget group increased, jumping significantly from 1982 onward. The amount distributed to the budget group did not fluctuate with changes in the retail price, whereas the amount distributed for open market sales was highly variable from year to year.

In Pakistan, wheat flour was distributed or sold by government-designated ration shops (retailers) as well as by private traders. The government sold wheat from its stocks to the mills to be processed into flour, and it sold flour to the government-appointed retailers. The retailers, in turn, sold flour at a fixed price to designated low-income consumers called "ration card holders." Wheat flour distributed by the ration shops constituted about 30 percent of Pakistan's total consumption throughout the 1970s and 1980s, until the rationing system was abolished in 1986/87. Except for one or two years, the share in total consumption of subsidized wheat distributed through the ration shops was larger than the share of wheat output procured. The stocks at the disposal of the government were procured from domestic markets as well as from imports.

The system of partially providing wheat to consumers, under a dual-pricing system in which the price of wheat sold to the mills from government stocks was considerably less than the open market price of wheat, was abolished in 1987. During 1986/87, the former price was about 30 percent less than the latter. By the 1980s, the shortcomings of the system were obvious: ration shops were not located all around the country; indeed 60 percent of the shops were concentrated in only two provinces. Also, the quality of flour provided at the ration shops was inferior to that available in the open market. Only 20 percent of the subsidized wheat supplied by the government to the flour mills was actually purchased by the consumers in the ration shops (Alderman, Chaudhry, and Garcia 1987). It became apparent that the primary beneficiaries of the system were not the consumers, but the flour millers, the ration shop owners, and the officials of the government distribution agency.

In 1987 a new system was introduced in which the government would sell wheat in the open market, not to ration card holders or mills, but to whoever wanted to buy wheat at a fixed price. The government was willing to sell unlimited quantities at this price. Under the old dual-pricing system, the subsidy on rationed wheat was about 30 percent, whereas under the new system of generalized subsidy, the rate of subsidy per ton was about 20 percent. Previously, there was a higher subsidy and a smaller number of designated consumers to whom the subsidized wheat was available. Under the new system, the amount of subsidy per ton was lower, but it covered a much wider population. The government undertook to sell unlimited quantities without any restrictions on the amount to be purchased by consumers. The difference between the sales price fixed by the government and the retail price in the market, however, was not more than 15 percent. Wheat sold by the government was generally of lower quality; the difference between the subsidized price and the open market price of the low-quality rice was thus small.

In Bangladesh, public distribution of foodgrains—both rice and wheat—took place through rationing and nonmarket channels such as food-for-work programs and various feeding and relief programs for the poorest segments of the population. Open market sales directly related to price stabilization only began in 1977. The total distribution of foodgrains through the subsidized rationing system as well as through feeding and food-for-work programs constituted no more than 11 to 15 percent of total consumption during 1977–80 and 11 to 14 percent during 1980–90. Participation of the poor in the nonmarket component of the food distribution system varied in response to fluctuations in open market prices. The higher the food prices in the open market, the greater was the impact on consumption by the poor and the greater was their need to participate in feeding programs. In any case, 85 percent of the publicly distributed food went through nonmarket channels during the 1970s; by the late 1980s and early 1990s, that proportion had increased to 37 percent and 63 percent went through market channels (Goletti 1993; Chowdhury and Shahabuddin 1992). By the late 1980s open market sales were 7.6 percent of the publicly distributed system, rising from 1 percent in 1977/78. It was noted, however, that ration shop purchases by low-income consumers varied in response to the price differences between open market and ration prices. In other words, when ration prices were significantly lower than market prices, there were increased purchases from the public distribution system.

Setting Procurement and Sales Prices

Price targets—floor support prices and ceiling prices—were explicitly stated in terms of nominal prices. In fixing these prices, however, the real prices that nominal prices would imply for producers and consumers were implicitly recognized. Instead of fixing floor and ceiling prices in real terms and deriving nominal prices for purchase and sales operations by a rigid formula, nominal prices were determined keeping in mind the notional real price. This was done by taking into account prices of inputs and other purchases by farmers, including the prices of crops competing in production. Similarly, in the determination of ceiling prices, income of the consumers and prices of other commodities bought by consumers were taken into account. But other prices relevant to producers or consumers were not related in a rigorous way to nominal prices, so as to yield a set of predetermined real prices as targets to be pursued by the public foodgrain agencies.

Procurement Price. How was the price at which procurement was undertaken by the public agency determined? If the objective of procurement was simply to secure supplies for the public food distribution system, there was no need to determine a procurement price different from what prevailed in the market. However, since the governments were interested in influencing market prices through procurement, the injection of an additional demand in the form of government procurement could be expected to raise the market price above what otherwise would have prevailed. Accordingly, the governments decided to have a "trigger price"—a target or procurement price—to start the process of procurement. Consequently, they offered a price that was different from the market price, in order to steer the market price toward the target. From the point of view of reducing the instability of prices, the procurement price provided the floor price or the lower bound of the range of price fluctuations.

Bangladesh, Pakistan, and the Philippines explicitly stated a number of factors that helped determine the procurement price. They included costs of production, especially the costs of purchased inputs; domestic demand and supply situation and prospects; foodgrain stocks; world market prices (export and import parity prices); prices of competing groups; and real income of farmers.

In the Philippines, special mention was made of the level of support prices obtaining in other countries. Among the prices of purchased inputs, the price of fertilizer received special mention in Indonesia and the Philippines. The rice-fertilizer price ratio was specially important in Indonesia during the 1970s and 1980s since the floor price of rice was considered a crucial incentive for stimulating domestic rice production. The procurement/floor price was fixed to ensure that the ratio of the fertilizer price to the rice price was adequate to encourage widespread use of fertilizer to increase rice production. The fertilizer price was subsidized by the government. Therefore, decisions on the rate of the fertilizer subsidy and the floor price were taken simultaneously. The higher the rate of subsidy on fertilizer and the lower the price of fertilizer, the lower the procurement price of rice required to provide incentive to the farmers for increased rice production. Rice and fertilizer prices were thus considered to be a set of complementary tools for improving food self-sufficiency. In the long run, the rice-fertilizer price ratio in Indonesia was regulated to reduce the burden of the fertilizer subsidy commensurate with the need to achieve food security. With the emergence of surplus rice stocks during the 1980s, fertilizer prices were raised to discourage production and hence to reduce excess supplies of rice. When rice stocks were large, increases in floor prices (nominal prices) were kept below the rate of inflation. For example, during the late 1980s, the strategy was to hold rice prices constant in real terms, while raising fertilizer prices. As a result, the reduction in incentives brought down the rate of growth in rice production during 1986 and 1987. By 1987, when shortages reappeared and prices tended to increase, stocks of foodgrains were large enough to constrain price rises.

It is important to recognize that in practice, the various factors mentioned above for determining the floor or procurement price were used mainly to make marginal adjustments in price from one year to the next. The decision facing the government in a particular year was whether to lower or raise the nominal procurement price below or above the previous year's procurement price and, if so, by how much. If a government was introducing a procurement system for the first time, the decision facing the government was how much to adjust last year's market price in order to determine the current procurement price. In both cases, the question was basically whether and how much to adjust the previous year's price. Second, the various factors that went into determination of the procurement price were not given quantitative weights in any of these countries. Decisions were based on officials' judgments and in some cases in an ad hoc manner. Over the years, however, a few countries sought to institutionalize the process of price determination by providing for interministerial or interagency consultation to decide on the procurement price; in others, semi-autonomous agricultural price commissions were established, with the authority to recommend procurement prices to the relevant ministry or the cabinet. In the end, the final decision was the result of negotiations and agreement among the various ministries or departments involved in promoting production of interrelated crops, or in the provision of supplies of agricultural inputs, or in imports and public distribution of food.

In Pakistan there has been an Agricultural Prices Commission since the 1980s, but no such commission exists in Bangladesh, Indonesia, or the Philippines, and the decision on the procurement price was left to interministerial consultations in those countries. In Bangladesh, the Ministry of Agriculture (in charge of policy relating to distribution of agricultural inputs, extension, education, and research and training, that is, programs designed to increase food production) and the Ministry of Food (in charge of the procurement operations, fixation of the targets of procurement, and public distribution of food) played key roles in determination of the procurement price. The Ministry of Food had an interest in larger procurement but not at a high price, since it adversely affected consumption of the beneficiaries of the food distribution system. The Ministry of Agriculture was interested in a high price in order to stimulate production.

The procurement price for rice in Bangladesh, Indonesia, and the Philippines was designed partly as an incentive for encouraging domestic production because rice was an import-substituting commodity; the case was similar for wheat in Bangladesh and Pakistan. In Pakistan and Thailand, where rice was an export commodity, the rice procurement price was designed to expand exports and, in addition, in Pakistan to earn profits for the export marketing organization.

Sales or Distribution Price. The prices at which the government marketing agencies sold foodgrains, either in the open market or to the designated consumers under the public distribution system, were determined in different ways in different countries. The public distribution system or open market sales by the public agency provided an alternative source of supplies for consumers. Thus, it affected the purchasers in the market and consequently prices. When market prices rose, purchases from the public agencies went up and upward pressure on market prices was reduced; when market prices went down the opposite occurred. In the Philippines, for example, the ceiling prices that triggered sales by the government in the market were determined partly on the basis of historical and expected price movements (the latter determined by the projected supply and demand) and partly on the basis of the price at which the marketing agency procured supplies from both imports and domestic production, including the costs of storage and distribution. In both Bangladesh and Pakistan, the ration prices at which sales were made to the designated consumers were partly related to historical price trends, income, purchasing power of low-income groups, the relative importance of wheat and rice in the food consumption basket, and the impact of cereal prices on their cost of living. Ration prices were also partly related to the procurement price and the amount of subsidy that the government wanted to provide. Since, in both countries, a large part of the public food distribution was intended for civilian and military employees of the government, the amount of food subsidy to be granted to them depended upon their weight in the political and administrative decisionmaking process. Insofar as the urban working classes—including industrial workers—in both countries received food subsidies through the public foodgrain distribution system, any increase in the ration price was likely to be linked to the demand for increases in urban industrial wages. Therefore, an important consideration in determining the ration price was its impact on the cost of living of urban workers and the need to constrain a rise in urban wages.

When open market sales were introduced in 1977 in Bangladesh, they were intended for lean seasons and were linked to the procurement price at harvest, with a margin of 15 percent in some areas and 20 percent in others. At the same time, they were linked to market prices. The open market sales prices were raised by one-half of every 10 percent increase in market prices. The objective was for the open market sales price to increase in response to the evolving supply and demand situation but not to the same extent as market prices. The open market sale prices were expected to remain below market prices and thus to dampen the rise in market prices when there was an imbalance between supply and demand.

In Indonesia, the food rations provided to the budget group were explicitly recognized to be a salary supplement or in lieu of an equivalent amount of cash salary. The price at which the food rations were evaluated, or the accounting price, was based on cost plus profit of the food marketing agency. While emphasis was placed on maintenance of interyear stability in real prices, the nominal ceiling price was decided internally by BULOG as the seasons progressed and might not be fixed at all if conditions did not warrant its publication. The objective of the exercise was to keep the traders guessing about the extent and timing of open market sales and thus to encourage a timely flow of private stocks into the market. Since the mid-1980s, BULOG has not announced a ceiling price at all; it has decided on a selling price when it makes sales in the open market to influence the retail price if it seems to be rising too fast (Ellis 1993a, 1993b).

Impact of Public Procurement and Distribution on Prices

The relative levels of procurement and support prices and market prices, on the one hand, and ceiling and retail prices, on the other, in different countries, are shown in Table 4. During the early 1970s and late 1980s,

Table 4—Ratio of farmgate to support prices and retail to ceiling prices, 1970–90

Year	Philippines FP/SP, Rice	Philippines RP/CP, Rice	Thailand FP/SP, Rice	Indonesia FP/SP, Rice	Indonesia RP/CP, Rice	Bangladesh FP/SP, Rice	Bangladesh RP/OMS, Rice	Bangladesh FP/SP, Wheat	Pakistan FP/SP, Wheat	Pakistan RP/CP, Wheat	Pakistan FP/SP, Basmati Rice
1970	1.21	1.53	n.a.	0.73	0.94	n.a.	n.a.	n.a.	0.97	n.a.	0.78
1971	1.44	2.05	n.a.	0.70	0.91	n.a.	n.a.	n.a.	0.96	1.43	0.81
1972	1.19	1.38	n.a.	0.76	0.90	0.87	n.a.	n.a.	0.97	1.51	0.82
1973	1.25	1.29	0.80	0.70	0.87	0.89	n.a.	n.a.	0.97	1.93	0.83
1974	1.15	1.03	0.77	0.67	0.91	1.20	n.a.	n.a.	0.97	2.36	0.86
1975	0.98	1.02	0.95	0.64	0.91	0.60	n.a.	0.78	0.97	2.29	0.84
1976	0.93	1.00	1.00	0.63	0.92	0.56	n.a.	1.07	0.96	1.61	0.84
1977	0.91	1.01	0.93	0.63	0.91	0.65	n.a.	0.99	0.96	1.48	0.83
1978	0.89	0.99	0.87	0.64	0.94	0.68	n.a.	0.94	0.97	1.62	0.84
1979	0.83	0.97	0.98	0.71	0.95	0.75	1.20	1.02	0.83	1.53	0.82
1980	0.84	0.98	0.77	0.69	0.84	0.60	1.01	0.99	0.96	1.30	0.83
1981	0.86	0.98	0.91	0.58	0.89	0.69	1.20	1.13	0.96	1.43	0.83
1982	0.83	0.99	n.a.	0.54	0.89	0.73	1.16	1.19	0.96	1.25	0.82
1983	0.87	0.99	n.a.	0.67	0.89	0.76	1.18	1.04	0.96	1.22	0.81
1984	0.94	1.10	n.a.	0.66	0.92	0.72	1.13	1.03	0.96	1.29	0.80
1985	0.94	1.16	n.a.	0.65	0.89	0.67	1.08	1.02	0.96	1.46	0.85
1986	0.81	1.19	n.a.	0.57	0.93	0.73	1.25	1.07	0.96	1.42	0.74
1987	0.84	1.20	n.a.	0.53	0.88	0.68	1.24	0.97	n.a.	1.18	n.a.
1988	0.91	1.36	n.a.	0.65	0.95	0.68	1.23	1.05	n.a.	1.22	n.a.
1989	1.08	1.48	n.a.	0.68	0.85	n.a.	1.11	n.a.	n.a.	1.20	n.a.
1990	0.92	1.38	n.a.	n.a.	0.88	n.a.	1.10	n.a.	n.a.	1.18	n.a.

Sources: Balisacan, Clarette, and Cortez 1992; Bangladesh Bureau of Statistics 1991; Chowdhury and Shahabuddin 1992; Pakistan, Finance Division 1992; Siamwalla et al. 1992; and Sudaryanto, Hermanto, and Pasandran 1992.

Notes: FP = farm price, SP = support price, RP = retail price, CP = ceiling price, and OMS = open market sales. For Pakistan and Bangladesh, the retail price of wheat is represented by the retail price of flour. n.a. is "not available."

retail prices in the Philippines were above the ceiling prices; during the late 1970s and early 1980s, retail prices were at par or below the ceiling price. This was partly the result of an increase in domestic rice production and imports. It was difficult to determine whether the public distribution of rice had any impact on the level of retail prices. The variation in the ratio of the public distribution of rice to total consumption was not closely related to the proximity or otherwise of the retail price to the ceiling price during these two years. The ratio of public distribution to total consumption was significantly high during the early 1980s, whereas it was as high during the early 1970s as during the late 1980s (Table 4). Without public distribution, it could be argued, the retail price might have diverged from the ceiling price to a greater extent than it did. Since 1984, there has been a widening of the gap between the retail price and the ceiling price, attributed to the adverse effects of bad weather on production, delayed imports, and a decline in the amount of rice released in the market by the National Food Authority.

At the same time, intervention by the National Food Authority to support the floor price was not successful in raising the market price to the level of the support price. Despite the procurement program, farm prices remained below the paddy support price for most of the years. For example, the expenditures of the National Food Authority in defense of the support price, estimated as the excess of the support price over the farmgate price multiplied by the amount of procurement, was only 21 percent of its budget—a rather small proportion—during 1988–91, whereas its expenditures on maintenance of the ceiling price, estimated as the excess of the retail price over the ceiling price multiplied by the amount of the publicly distributed rice, constituted about 83 percent of its budget (Table 4). From the point of view of the expenditures incurred by the National Food Authority, the focus of the stabilization policy was on price paid by consumers rather than on supporting prices received by producers (Balisacan, Clarette, and Cortez 1992). Toward the end of the 1980s, the divergence between the retail and the release ceiling prices widened: that is, retail prices rose significantly above the ceiling prices. This meant that, under the circumstances, the National Food Authority could have been self-financing if it had sold rice at market prices instead of selling rice to private traders well below the market prices. Thus, the government support to the National Food Authority was tantamount in practice to subsidies to private wholesale dealers rather than being used to support price stabilization.

In Indonesia, the procurement operations were unable to raise the producer's price up to or beyond the level of the floor price in any year. On the other hand, retail prices were almost always below the ceiling prices. The government stock policy seems to have succeeded in keeping retail prices low and stable.

In Pakistan, the procurement price of wheat was almost always higher than the producer's price. The retail price of flour outside the rationing system was 30 to 40 percent above the ration price until 1986/87. It was only after 1975/76, as the burden of subsidies mounted steeply, that prices charged at the ration shops were increased somewhat. In the 1980s, burdened with heavy subsidies, ration shop prices and prices for sale to the mills were raised significantly. After the abolition of the rationing system, the difference between the open market sale price and the retail price was substantially reduced, partly because of the quality differential. The total amount of subsidy to wheat flour was as high as 8 percent of government expenditures during 1978/79 and gradually declined over the years as ration prices were adjusted upward. By late 1985/86, this ratio declined to 3 percent (Alderman, Chaudhry, and Garcia 1988).

In Bangladesh, in most of the years, the farmers' rice price was below the support price, and the retail price was higher than the open market sale price. In one period, 1977/78 to 1987/88, in 14 out of 22 cases during the main harvest months (November–December for *aman* and May–June for *boro*), producer prices were below procurement prices. The difference was as high as 30 percent during the bumper *boro* crop of 1980/81 (Chowdhury and Shahabuddin 1992).

The ration price of rice was 45 to 60 percent of the retail price during the 1970s. Due to a gradual increase in the ration price during the 1980s, it was 69 to 78 percent of the retail price (Chowdhury 1989). In the case of wheat, the retail price was between 56 and 78 percent during the 1970s and it was 80 percent of the retail price during the 1980s. The budgetary subsidy that was provided to the food distribution system was quite high, doubling between the mid-1970s and mid-1980s (World Bank 1990, Attachment 32). However, under the pressure of budgetary constraints beginning in the mid-1980s, there was a decrease in the amount of subsidy as a result of a rise in the ration price and a reduction in the amount of public distribution. As the difference between the ration price and the retail price narrowed, the amount distributed through rationing and open market sales was also reduced. The share of food subsidy in the government's revenue and current expenditure rose as high as 14 percent during 1981/82. It was significantly reduced at the end of the 1980s—4.0 percent in 1986/87, rising to 10.4 percent in 1989/90 (World Bank 1993).

Effectiveness of Public Stocks Policy in Stabilizing Prices

The effectiveness of procurement operations and open market sales in raising the price paid to farmers to the level of the support price or in restraining the retail price to keep it below the ceiling price has varied among countries and in the same country over time. The effectiveness of the price support program in defending floor or ceiling prices depends on a number of closely interrelated factors, including, first, whether a wide enough gap exists between the ceiling and the floor prices, and whether private stocks held by traders and farmers play a supporting role—that is, the extent to which private stocks are important and whether or how much private traders engage in speculation to counter the expected government stock operations. Second, the effectiveness of the program depends on whether public stocks are adequately managed (with proper timing of procurement and release of stocks) and on whether adequate and flexible finance arrangements are available.

The gap between the ceiling and floor prices is important for two reasons. First, it determines the amount of subsidy required by the public agency for implementing ceiling and floor prices. Second, it affects the role that private trade plays in foodgrain distribution—the extent to which private stocks supplement or supplant public stockholding. A wide margin between the floor and the ceiling price, which covers the costs of private stocks and permits them to make a profit, encourages private stockholding, thus reducing the amount of public stocks that are required. The larger the margin, the larger the degree of price fluctuation that can be tolerated as a matter of policy. Any attempt to keep the margin wide enough to cover the costs of private stocks, while keeping a low ceiling price, can only succeed if the floor price is also kept low. This would have adverse effects on production incentives.

While the National Food Authority in the Philippines considered the milling and transportation costs explicitly when setting floor and ceiling prices, the cost of storage was ignored. Price margins were barely wide enough to cover the costs of storage alone in two years, 1972/73 and 1980/81 (Unnevehr 1985). Marketing margins were slow to adjust to changes in marketing costs. On average, they were about 47 percent during the 1970s and continued to decline thereafter (Umali 1985). Because the government placed priority on maintaining low consumer prices, downward pressure was exerted on paddy procurement prices in order to cover the marketing costs.

The gap between the procurement and release prices in the Philippines was often set by the National Food Authority without regard to marketing costs, in order to meet the conflicting objectives of providing high prices to producers and low prices to consumers. There was no incentive for private traders to participate since the price margin was too narrow to allow for the full recovery of private marketing costs, especially transportation costs. Thus, the National Food Authority was left with no competition. And because its trading costs were higher than those of the private traders, the government had to subsidize the trading operations of the agency. At the same time, the government wanted to maintain a role for private trade and provided incentives to private traders through subsidized loan programs. The subsidized loans were offered to rice traders under two different programs presumably to lower private marketing costs. One program made loans at 10 percent annual interest with stocks bonded by the National Food Authority as security. Another program under the Development Bank of the Philippines included loans for investment in rice milling and provided working capital for storage at 14 to 18 percent annual interest. A more efficient way of reducing marketing costs would have been investment in transportation and communication infrastructure or enactment of policies to encourage growth of financial institutions for financing private trade.

In Indonesia, the margin between the floor and ceiling price was determined primarily with reference to the storage and distribution costs incurred by the private sector. The margin changed over the years in response to changes in marketing conditions and costs in transporta-

Table 5—Marketing margin for rice in Indonesia

Plan	Period	Percentage Difference Between Ceiling and Floor Prices[a]
		(percent)
Plan II	1974/75 – 1978/79	17 – 46
Plan III	1979/80 – 1981/82	11 – 23
Plan IV	1982/83 – 1983/84	31 – 34
Plan V	1984/85 – 1988/89	30 – 56

Source: Atmaja, Amat, and Sidik 1989.
[a]The percentages given are for the lowest and highest prices during the period.

tion, storage, and marketing. Because the ratio between the ceiling and the floor prices has widened in recent years (Table 5), the marketing agency has needed a smaller subsidy.

Private traders played a larger role than in other countries in stockholding and in seasonal trading to even out price fluctuations. The role of the private sector in storage is evident from the fact that 50 percent of the peak season surplus was carried over into deficit seasons by traders and 30 percent by farmers, whereas only 20 percent was carried over by BULOG as public procurement (Ellis 1993b). However, in Indonesia, as in the Philippines, there was pressure from time to time to narrow the margin to ease the dilemma of how to provide low prices for consumers and price incentives for producers. Because the private sector handled such a large share of the rice market in Indonesia, any decision to reduce or compress the marketing margin was tantamount to a decision to squeeze the private sector and consequently to place a proportionately greater burden on public stock operations.

In Pakistan, from the late 1960s to the mid-1970s the price of flour at ration shops was not much above the price at which wheat was released to the mills from government stocks for processing into flour; nor was it much above the price at which the government procured wheat for eventual sale to the mills (Table 6). From time to time, the government attempted to reduce the amount of subsidy by raising the ration price of flour to keep it in line with increases in the procurement price of wheat. But in most cases, an increase in flour prices was tied to

Table 6—Wheat procurement price, sales price to mills, and ration shop price in Pakistan, 1981/82 to 1985/86

Price	1981/82	1982/83	1983/84	1984/85	1985/86
			(Rs/metric ton)		
Procurement price	1,450.0	1,600.0	1,600.0	1,750.0	1,750.0
Sales price to mills	1,567.4	1,702.9	1,702.9	1,702.9	1,702.9
Ration shop price	1,661.1	1,799.9	1,799.9	1,799.9	1,799.9

Source: Alderman et al. 1988.

an increase in wages for industrial workers rather than to the costs of marketing and distribution. The government absorbed the entire cost of storage, handling, and distribution through subsidy. Throughout the 1970s and 1980s the private sector could not compete with the public sector in wheat trade because of the large subsidy accruing to the public sector. The retail price of flour in the open market (outside of the rationing system) was considerably higher than the procurement price. Thus, the government share of the wheat trade began to expand, and by 1982 it reached a record high—73 percent of the marketable surplus in the Punjab (Naqvi and Burney 1992). Thus, an agency that was initially established to assure a minimum price to farmers ended up monopolizing wheat trading and marketing, squeezing out the private traders. There was a wide disparity between import and export parity prices for wheat during this period. During 1981 the import parity price exceeded the export parity price by about 50 percent; by 1986, the margin had widened to about 100 percent. The gap between import and export parity prices far exceeded the cost of handling and storing wheat between seasons—the latter being half of the former.

A comparable situation prevailed in Bangladesh in that the margin between the procurement price and the ration price of rice, or open-market sales price, initiated in the mid-1970s, was not high enough to cover the costs of storage, marketing, and distribution. Until the end of the 1970s, the ration price was below the procurement price; from 1980 on, the ration price was gradually increased, and by 1990 the ration price was only 6 to 7 percent higher than the procurement price. The situation in wheat was similar. The ration price was below the procurement price in the early years, but by the late 1980s and early 1990s, it was about 10 percent above the procurement price, even though it fell far short of the costs of storage, handling, and transportation. When open market sales at higher-than-ration prices were introduced in the mid-1970s, they exceeded the procurement price by no more than 17 percent in the early 1980s and 12 to 16 percent in the early 1990s. By the late 1990s, open market sales prices exceeded the procurement price by no more than 6 percent (World Bank 1991). There were occasions in the early 1990s when the government had to turn over its own rice stocks within three to four months or risk deterioration in the quality of stocks, even though seasonal price swings did not warrant intervention. To this extent, therefore, public stock operations were destabilizing the market price fluctuations. Frequently, in order to get rid of surplus stock, the government had to reduce the sales price and sustain budgetary losses. This, in turn, reduced the incentive for private storage.

Adequacy and Flexibility of Financing of Buffer Stock Operations

In Bangladesh, Pakistan, and the Philippines, the food stabilization agencies received annual budgetary allocations for carrying out procurement and open market sale operations. The allocations were provided in advance and were not related to the actual scale of procurement operations that were undertaken, which were frequently different from what was anticipated. In Indonesia, however, BULOG received a flexible line of credit on which it could draw according to its requirements and in response to fluctuations in prices or output.

In Indonesia and the Philippines, the food stabilization agencies were allowed to derive additional income from subsidiary activities in which they were engaged, apart from direct budgetary allocations. In the Philippines, the National Food Authority partly met the costs of subsidy, incurred when marketing costs exceeded sales proceeds, from profits derived from its trading activities in wheat, yellow corn, and flour. These commodities were imported duty-free by the National Food Authority and were sold in the domestic market at prices above the border prices.

In Indonesia, BULOG's profit from other trading operations was a significant source of financing for the costs incurred in its buffer stock operations. The agency was the monopoly importer of wheat and sugar, as well as the sole distributor in the domestic wheat flour and sugar market, either imported or domestically produced. It was also responsible for regulating and licensing imports and domestic marketing of soybeans. The relative importance of different commodities in BULOG's trading operations can be seen in Table 7.

The food agencies in Bangladesh, Pakistan, and the Philippines had access to bank credit in addition to direct budgetary allocations, often at subsidized interest rates. But this access to credit was not open-ended or predetermined on the basis of a line of credit. In the Philippines, the National Food Authority received credit from the Central Bank, but an open line of credit was not provided in advance, as in Indonesia. In most years, about half of the subsidy needed to cover the losses of the National Food Authority was met from the subsidy on interest rates that it paid.

In Indonesia, the magnitude of government procurements from the market and the release of foodgrains to the market were not the only factors that affected the success of the stabilization policy. The timing of purchases and sales were also crucial in order to gain credibility with the private traders as well as the farmers. Erratic timing tended to undermine confidence and to reduce the impact of the buffer stock operations on the market price. An efficient market intelligence system and sophis-

Table 7—Relative importance of different commodities in trading operations in Indonesia, 1988/89

Commodity	Supply (Stock and Procurement)	Marketing and Distribution
	(1,000 metric tons)	
Wheat flour	1,291.0	1,246.0
Sugar	2,591.0	2,327.0
Maize	48.6	48.2
Soybeans	649.0	506.0

Source: Atmaja, Amat, and Sidik 1989.

ticated import and purchase operations were important ingredients in the success of the Indonesian foodgrain stabilization agency. These prerequisites for efficient buffer stock operations were built gradually from the 1960s on and greatly improved over time.[11]

In the Philippines, over the entire period, insufficient or untimely imports sometimes tended to aggravate rather than to reduce seasonal price fluctuations. The procurement and release prices in the Philippines were announced by the government at random intervals and not well in advance of planting time; this made the government's actions highly unpredictable and adversely affected both short-term production and long-term investment decisions by the rice farmers. In Indonesia, floor prices were announced every year in October for the main harvest to be obtained in the following May. This announcement was made far ahead of planting and harvest time and at the same time every year to provide predictability and to influence planting decisions. In Indonesia, BULOG's imports were regular and timed to combat price pressures. Because their purchase operations had a sophisticated market intelligence system they were well timed and generally effective.

The possibility of speculative action on the part of private traders requires that at any given time the public agency must have stocks adequate to defend floor or ceiling prices. Without the possibility of speculation, public stocks could be smaller. Speculators can frustrate the work of a public agency if their price expectations differ from the government's. Therefore, it is important that the public agency pursue a credible purchase and sales policy, so that traders or potential stockholders can expect prices in the future to move in line with the government's projections. Not only must the public agency command sufficient resources to enable it to engage in market operations to bring prices into line, but it must also implement its decisions effectively and expeditiously. Note, however, that the resources at the disposal of an agency do not always have to be used. What is needed is the confidence and the perception in the public mind, especially among traders and farmers, that government not only has enough financial, administrative, and logistical capacity to successfully intervene but will in fact intervene if necessary. Therefore, the resources available "on call" may be large, but they will seldom be used to their fullest extent. The price projections or announcements by the government should not cover a long period, because they could go wrong, thus eroding credibility. Speculation concerning the floor or ceiling prices set by the government for the next period (season or year as the case may be) might frustrate the government's objective during the current period. Thus, the government

---

[11]BULOG's offices were scattered throughout the country; there were 27 provincial depots—one in each province—and 94 offices in the districts, employing 7,000 people during the late 1980s (Ellis 1993a). Each office collected producer and retail prices on a weekly basis, which were transmitted to headquarters by telex. Wholesale prices for rice were collected on a daily basis in the capital city. The summary price information was supplied to the management of BULOG on a daily basis.

cannot allow movements in price from one period to the next to be so high as to induce speculative storage in the first period. If the prices in government outlets or storage of government operations were stickier than the open market, the public storage authorities would have to contend not only with harvest fluctuations but also with large swings in demand as consumers switched back and forth between the public outlets and the open market.

Price Stabilization Policies in Exporting Countries

Pakistan and Thailand represent two cases where the foodgrains whose domestic prices are to be stabilized are also export commodities. Thailand is a major exporter of rice; therefore, it is assumed that elasticity of export demand is low, especially since the world market consists of only a few exporters. Pakistan, on the other hand, is not a large rice exporter, but it exports a particular variety of rice that commands a specialized market in a limited number of countries in West Asia and the Near East. During the period of this study, the export price was often negotiated bilaterally on a government-to-government basis, particularly in Pakistan, although government-to-government trade in Thailand until the 1970s was significant. In Thailand, rice is a major export commodity, an important item in the domestic consumption basket, and a major source of rural income. In Pakistan, rice is neither an important source of farmers' income (wheat is the major foodgrain), nor an important item in the consumption basket of Pakistani consumers. Assuming a low elasticity of export demand in a noncompetitive world market, both countries sought to maximize their export earnings by ensuring a high export price and driving a wedge between domestic and export prices.

Public Procurement, Support Prices, and Exports in Pakistan

Pakistan produces two main types of rice: Basmati rice and the varieties developed by the International Rice Research Institute (IRRI). At the time of this study, the IRRI varieties accounted for 60 percent of total rice production, while the Basmati variety accounted for about 30 percent; other minor varieties accounted for the remaining 10 percent. In early years, Basmati rice held the largest share of rice exports. Prior to 1977, the Pakistan Rice Export Corporation monopolized both domestic and foreign trade in rice. After 1977, while the monopoly in foreign trade was retained, the monopoly in domestic trade was abolished. However, compulsory procurement of rice was maintained, especially in Punjab, which is the major rice-producing area in the country. Voluntary procurement existed in Sindh, the next most important rice-producing province.

After 1977, there was compulsory procurement of rice from producers but no monopoly procurement: that is, rice producers were permitted to sell to private traders or buyers once the monthly procurement target was met at a predetermined procurement price of the Rice Export Corporation. In other words, the producers, including the privately owned rice mills, could sell whatever surplus remained. Prior to 1977, most of the rice mills were publicly owned; after 1977, they were privatized. Consequently, after 1977 the private rice mills directly or through intermediaries bought rice from the producers. Also, the Rice Export Corporation regulated the activities of private traders through a wide variety of measures such as licensing of rice dealers and mill owners, control of movement of rice between different provinces, allocation of quotas to dealers who could sell in the domestic market, and inspections of rice for quality control. Following the elimination of the Rice Export Corporation's monopoly procurement in 1977, the allocation and enforcement of quotas for sales in the domestic market by private rice dealers was the major instrument through which the corporation controlled domestic sales of rice and, therefore, wholesale prices in the domestic market.

The procurement price for rice in Pakistan was set at a level that could provide economic incentives to farmers by ensuring that farmers' prices were protected against the effects of fluctuations in world prices and that their costs of production were covered. In determining the support price of rice in Pakistan, export parity prices as well as adequate returns to farmers were taken into consideration.

In 1986, however, the Pakistani government abandoned its policy of compulsory procurement and introduced a system of voluntary procurement at a predetermined support or procurement price. As sales and delivery to the government procurement centers became voluntary, a free market was allowed to operate for domestic sales. However, the monopoly on export trade by the Rice Export Corporation continued until 1987. After 1987, private exports of Basmati rice were allowed in small packages, although the bulk exports remained a monopoly of the Rice Export Corporation. An extremely high export tax on private exports prevented any significant volume of exports by the private sector until 1990. Subsequently, rice exports were further liberalized, export duties were abolished, and bulk exports of Basmati rice were allowed in the private sector. Exports of IRRI rice varieties by the private sector have also been allowed since 1991.

The system of purchases or procurement of the Rice Export Corporation within the domestic market was tantamount to a price support program like that of wheat. Two levels of support prices were set annually. One was the paddy support price for farmers and the other was a support price for purchase from the rice millers where the Rice Export Corporation bought rice for export. Increasingly, however, the Rice Export Corporation focused on buying rice from mills rather than paddy from farmers, in view of the high administrative and logistic burden of on-farm procurement of paddy. The paddy support prices, which were announced each year prior to the planting season, served as a guide for millers and private traders.

Until 1986/87, the domestic wholesale price of rice (both IRRI and Basmati varieties) was higher than the producer's or procurement price; in fact, the excess of the wholesale price over the procurement price of rice was much higher than that in the case of wheat. Until 1977, the compulsory and monopoly procurement of rice by the Rice Export Corporation, which was intended mainly for exports, included a very small amount of sales in the domestic market; after 1977, when monopoly procurement was abolished but compulsory procurement was retained, whatever residual amount was left with the farmers could be sold in the domestic market. This, combined with restrictions on the amount of sales by private traders in the domestic market, kept domestic wholesale prices higher than the procurement price. This policy succeeded in driving a wedge between low producer prices, on the one hand, and high consumer prices, on the other, keeping domestic rice consumption low.

After 1987, when compulsory procurement was abolished, the Rice Export Corporation had to raise its procurement prices in order to compete in the open market with the private traders and to obtain adequate quantities of rice for export purposes. The procurement prices of both varieties increased significantly each year from 1987–89 onward. Even before 1986/87, procurement prices had to be raised on several occasions to discourage the unauthorized diversion of sales of rice to the private traders by producers. Export prices were, however, kept even higher than wholesale prices by restricting exports through the public monopoly of exports and later by the imposition of export taxes, quotas, and levies on private exports of Basmati rice. At the same time, the government still had the monopoly of the IRRI varieties of rice exports. In the late 1980s, faced with weak world demand, procurement prices for IRRI rice were raised above the export prices in order to prevent a serious fall in farmers' income.

Impact on Price Instability

Reduction of the variability of domestic wholesale prices was not the major aim of Pakistan's rice stabilization policy. Rather, the policy was designed to achieve a stable, high export price to maximize foreign exchange earnings. The procurement and wholesale prices for both the Basmati and IRRI rice increased over time, and procurement prices did not fluctuate much from year to year. The stability of the farmers' price was due in the early years to monopoly procurement by the public agency and later to compulsory procurement that left only a small amount for private traders. There was no ceiling price fixed for rice in the Pakistani market because there was no great concern about stabilizing consumer prices of rice in view of its negligible importance in the consumption basket of Pakistani consumers.

As mentioned earlier, the producer or wholesale price of rice was consistently higher than the government procurement price between 1977 and 1986. For Basmati rice, the excess ranged from 54 to 66 percent, and for IRRI rice, from 21 to 28 percent. A high degree of fluctuation in domestic wholesale prices was the result of the limited domestic market for rice. Fluctuations in exports were the main cause of fluctuations in wholesale prices of rice. Until the 1970s, exports of rice did not constitute a significant proportion of output. The impact of procurement on the farmers' price as well as on the domestic wholesale price was felt significantly only after the 1970s. During the 1980s, the ratio of procurement to production for rice of both kinds ranged from 25 to 41 percent. In recent years, the volume of stocks of rice held by the Rice Export Corporation increased significantly, as procurement increased consistently, because output expanded rapidly during the 1980s. At the same time, the ratio of exports to production declined from 46 percent in 1985/86 to 23 percent in 1989/90 (Pakistan, Finance Division 1992). Therefore, the variation in export volume was offset partly by an inverse variation in public stocks, so that the impact on the domestic wholesale prices was moderated.

The Rice Export Corporation incurred a loss on IRRI rice exports every year except 1988/89. Although profits were earned on Basmati rice exports, they could not wholly compensate for losses on the sale of the IRRI rice. The profits of the Export Corporation were further reduced because of inefficiencies in transportation, handling, and storage of rice. The cost of storage and handling was estimated to be as high as one-third of the Basmati price and one-half of the IRRI price. Therefore, the export and price stabilization operations undertaken by the Rice Export Corporation required heavy subsidies from the government.

Thailand: Variable Export Tax, Export Premium, and Resource Requirements

Thailand attempted to maintain stable, low domestic prices of rice by driving a wedge between its export price/world price and domestic price by means of export taxes of various kinds. In Thailand, rice is the principal cereal for domestic consumption. Thailand aimed to transmit to the world market the effects of fluctuations in domestic production; at the same time, it tried to moderate the impact of fluctuations in world supplies and prices on domestic prices. This was done by adjusting the various components of the regime of export taxation in response to external price fluctuations or domestic supply variations. As a major exporter of rice, Thailand could have contributed to the stability of the world price by increasing exports at times of shortages in the world market and reducing them during world surpluses, but it chose not to do so. Instead, it tried to stabilize domestic prices at the expense of instability in world prices. During shortages in the world market, when prices were high, export taxes were raised and exports were restricted to prevent a rise in domestic prices; during periods of low prices in the world market, export taxes were lowered.

The export control regime in Thailand consisted of two types of export taxes: an export tax, including an export premium, and rice reserve requirements imposed upon the rice exporters as a percentage of their exports. The net burden on exports due to the combination of the three provisions amounted to 28 percent in 1981; it was reduced to 5.3 percent in 1983. The export premium was in fact a specific tax, whereas the export tax was an ad valorem tax. The export tax could not be changed easily without the consent of the Parliament, whereas the export premium could be changed by administrative action of the Ministry of Commerce. The export premium was tantamount to a fee to be paid by private rice exporters to obtain a license to export. Thus it served both as an instrument of quantitative control on exports as well as a tax on exports. On the assumption that export demand was inelastic, it was expected that the burden would be borne predominantly by foreign buyers; in fact, during the period 1960–85, domestic price was on the whole no more than 40 percent of the f.o.b. export price.

Both the export tax and the export premium were important sources of revenue during the 1950s and 1960s. In the earlier years, the export premium was a much bigger source of revenue than the export tax. Because it was a predominant source of government revenue in those years, it was not feasible to change the premium without destabilizing the government's budget. Hence, the export premium seldom varied except in the late 1970s and late 1980s. Fortunately for Thailand, during the 1950s and 1960s, the world market in rice was relatively stable; the occasions when the export tax and premium needed to be changed to stabilize the domestic price were few. Only in recent years, with greater world price fluctuations, has the need for changes in the export taxes and premiums to achieve domestic price stability become important. At the same time, the use of export taxes and premiums as stabilizing instruments suffered limitations; while taxes could be varied up or down, there was no scope for a subsidy or a negative tax during a period of surplus or low prices. Second, neither tax varied automatically in relation to a ceiling or a floor price. In other words, there was no threshold price, which, if the cereal price rose above it, the export tax would rise. Conversely, if the price fell below the threshold, the export tax would fall. Each time, a discretionary change had to be made, usually in the export premium rather than the export tax, because the premium was administratively a more flexible instrument. Variations in the export premium within and between years are shown in Table 8.

Table 8—Annual and interannual variations in the export premium for paddy in Thailand

Period	Range
	(B/metric ton)
1960–66	500–550
1966–67	550–950
1970–72	340–530
1973	530
1974	2,410
1975	884
1976–77	360–368
1978–79	510
1980–82	201–482
1983–84	100–176

Source: Siamwalla and Setboonsarng 1989.

During the 1960s and 1970s, export taxation consisting of the different types of levies performed well as a stabilizer of prices. During this period, the world rice price was volatile and the domestic price varied less than the world price. In the early 1980s, a global decline in world food prices brought down the export price of rice, and this led to a decrease in the rates of rice premiums over time. The export premium was abolished in 1986, but the export tax continued until 1990.

Under the system of rice reserve requirements that began early in the 1960s, exporters were required to sell a fixed share of exports (known as the rice reserve requirement ratio) to the government at prices set below market prices. Rice reserve requirements were changed not only from year to year but also several times within a year, varying in response to changes in domestic prices in relation to export prices. In fact, it operated as a variable levy. The private exporters acquired stocks or had more to export when reserve requirements were reduced because domestic supplies were plentiful and prices were low. The reserve requirements were raised as domestic prices went up, while the food stocks obtained by the government were released in the domestic market to contain a rise in consumer prices.

The extent of variation in reserve requirements is seen in Table 9. In the early years when public storage capacity was limited, instead of requiring that stocks be physically delivered, the government accepted an obligation from exporters to provide supplies to the government whenever needed, so that it could release them in the market. This shifted the burden of holding stocks from the government to the exporters. However, many exporters decided not to hold stocks but to buy supplies in the market for delivery when they were required by the government. Since this was usually when prices were rising, this system added to the upward pressure on domestic price and aggravated rather than moderated price rises in times of scarcity. The system of reserve requirements was abolished in 1982.

Reserve requirements also served as a mechanism for obtaining rice at or below market prices so that the amount procured could be distributed, if needed, by the government to urban consumers. The subsidy provided to the consumers was no more than 10 percent below the open market price, and the burden of the subsidy was borne by the exporters rather than by the general tax revenues of the government.

The distribution of rice obtained through reserve requirements was predominantly confined to the city of Bangkok. In 1977, 80 percent of the rice procured by the government was distributed to consumers in Bangkok; by 1982, Bangkok's share had declined to 45 percent and the distribution to outlying areas was increased.

With the increase in world prices, the rate of consumer subsidy in relation to the retail price increased from 10 percent during 1966–68 to 25–30 percent during 1973–74 (Panayotou 1989b). By the mid-1970s, the leakage of subsidized rice had become a big problem. The rice reserve was resold by the government to selected shops for sale to urban consumers at a low price. The amount of rice allowed per transaction was fixed, but there was no limit to the number of transactions. There was no way the government could determine the amount of rice

Table 9—Price variability and its explanatory factors

Country/Crop/Period	Variability				Procurement Ratio	Distribution Ratio
	Wholesale Price	Production	Imports or Exports	Retail Price		
Pakistan (wheat)						
1961–65	0.06	0.11	0.36	n.a.	0.50	n.a.
1966–70	0.16	0.13	0.68	n.a.	11.88	n.a.
1971–75	0.15	0.03	0.51	0.11	12.73	26.00
1976–80	0.05	0.06	0.73	0.05	21.40	30.40
1981–85	0.01	0.07	0.58	0.02	26.15	30.40
1986–90	0.09	0.05	0.76	0.07	31.14	n.a.
Philippines (rice)						
1961–65	0.05	n.a.	n.a.	0.08	n.a.	n.a.
1966–70	0.04	0.04	1.26	0.08	2.93	n.a.
1971–75	0.10	0.08	0.83	0.03	0.61	8.00
1976–80	0.12	0.03	1.06	0.09	7.64	4.70
1981–85	0.06	0.04	3.62	0.07	6.13	8.60
1986–90	0.05	0.03	4.01	0.04	4.30	8.10
Bangladesh (rice)						
1971–75	0.38	0.06	0.24	0.38	1.50	2.50
1976–80	0.11	0.03	0.74	0.13	3.40	4.70
1981–85	0.04	0.02	0.79	0.08	1.30	3.40
1986–90	0.09	0.04	0.68	0.11	2.70	3.50
Bangladesh (wheat)						
1971–75	0.47	0.30	0.36	n.a.	n.a.	91.20
1976–80	0.05	0.18	0.36	n.a.	12.11	95.00
1981–85	0.03	0.12	0.28	n.a.	8.81	67.30
1986–90	0.08	0.04	0.35	n.a.	7.74	68.40

(continued)

Table 9—Continued

Country/Crop/Period	Variability				Procurement Ratio	Distribution Ratio
	Wholesale Price	Production	Imports or Exports	Retail Price		
Indonesia (rice)						
1971–75	0.26	0.05	0.35	0.11	2.93	7.80
1976–80	0.06	0.03	0.43	0.03	4.12	10.60
1981–85	0.03	0.02	0.86	0.06	7.42	8.40
1986–90	0.06	0.02	0.42	0.07	5.65	6.90
Pakistan (rice)						
1961–65	0.19	0.18	0.67	0.06	n.a.	n.a.
1966–70	0.18	0.13	0.21	0.17	n.a.	n.a.
1971–75	0.21	0.04	0.38	0.18	20.28	n.a.
1976–80	0.09	0.04	0.11	0.04	32.50	n.a.
1981–85	0.06	0.07	0.20	0.07	35.55	n.a.
1986–90	0.09	0.04	0.23	0.07	34.47	n.a.
Thailand (rice)						
1961–65	0.09	0.14	0.46	n.a.	n.a.	n.a.
1966–70	0.10	0.09	0.25	n.a.	n.a.	n.a.
1971–75	0.19	0.05	0.26	n.a.	n.a.	n.a.
1976–80	0.02	0.06	0.17	n.a.	n.a.	n.a.
1981–85	0.13	0.05	0.11	n.a.	n.a.	n.a.
1986–90	0.15	0.05	0.09	n.a.	n.a.	n.a.

Sources: Balisacan, Clarette, and Cortez 1992; Bangladesh, Bureau of Statistics 1991; Chowdhury and Shahabuddin 1992; Pakistan, Finance Division 1992; Siamwalla et al. 1992; and Sudaryanto, Hermanto, and Pasandran 1992.

Notes: Variability is measured by the standard deviation for five-year periods of the percentage differences between trends and actual values of respective variables. The procurement ratio is the average ratio of procurement to production. The distribution ratio is the average ratio of public distribution to consumption. n.a. is "not available."

required by each shop. A substantial proportion of subsidized rice, therefore, was alleged to have been resold to the free market.

The distribution of rice from the reserve stocks of the government was not focused toward any particular income group either in Bangkok or elsewhere in Thailand. For example, there was no policy that rice should be distributed only to low-income consumers. In fact, the way the distribution of rice was carried out possibly discriminated against the poor. The buyers had to show identity cards as well as proof of registration in the districts in which they were buying. These requirements ruled out the poor consumers who did not have identity cards and recent immigrants to the city who had not yet registered or changed their addresses.

The price subsidy program was supported by the retailers for the obvious reason that the government allowed them to charge a comfortable margin of profit included in the selling price. Also, it was possible to sell stocks in the open market at prices higher than what the government allowed. There was no way the government could detect or prevent illegal selling below the officially determined price.

The Public Procurement and Price Support Program in Thailand

Starting in the 1970s, a small price support program was introduced by the government. Two organizations were involved in implementing it: the Marketing Organization for Farmers (MOF), run by the Ministry of Agriculture, and the Public Warehouse Organization (PWO), run by the Ministry of Commerce. The purpose of the MOF was to buy paddy from the farmers at the support price, while the PWO was to procure rice from the rice mills at the support price. The program was financed by the Farmers' Aid Fund, which received in its turn resources from the proceeds of the export premium. In addition to the Farmers' Aid Fund, the profits from the government-to-government trade were a source of finance that accrued to the Ministry of Commerce and therefore could be used by the PWO.

Under the systems of rice reserve requirements and price supports, the burden of the consumer subsidy was borne by both the rice exporters and rice farmers. The prices paid for procurement from the exporters and the farmers, as well as the resale price paid by the government to the retailers, were fixed so that there was no burden on the government budget. The price support program was ineffective. Except in years of strong demand and high world prices—such as 1976/77, 1977/78, and 1980/81—farm prices were always below support prices. Furthermore, in most years, procurement was about 1 percent of production; only during the years of considerable surplus, 1980/81 and 1981/82, did procurement reach as high as 11 to 12 percent of production. Even in these years, farm prices were only 77 percent of support prices. This was partly because purchases were untimely and partly because funds were inadequate. The lack of funds, the limited public storage capacity, and delays in decisionmaking processes regarding the need for price supports, as well as the inappropriate timing of purchases, all mitigated against the success of the procurement programs. Delays in deciding to undertake purchases meant that many farmers were compelled by their immediate need for cash and debt-service payment to sell their crop to traders. The traders in their turn benefited from the price support program by selling to the government agencies at the procurement price. Also, the limited and uncertain allocation of funds by the government kept the amount of procurement low. Because of lack of funds and limited public storage capacity, stocks of rice could not be held for long and were often released to the market soon after they were procured.

Few farmers were able to sell paddy to the government agency because the transaction cost of buying paddy from farmers was very high. Eventually, the government agency turned to purchasing paddy from rice millers. Large quantities of paddy were purchased and stored by the millers, who had the skill and the storage capacity to act as agents for the price support program. This resulted in a transfer of income from the government to the millers, but it was not much help in raising paddy prices at harvest time for farmers. The farmers received only 30 percent of the amount dispensed under the price support program, whereas 87 percent went to intermediaries such as millers, exporters, farmers' organizations, officials, and politicians. Moreover, the farmers who benefited from the program were mostly the large commercial farmers (Panayotou 1989a).

Even though both the rice subsidy and the price support programs were small, inadequately funded, and relatively ineffective, they were politically popular. The retail shop owners and the rice millers, who were the principal beneficiaries, were among the strongest supporters. The price support program was popular with the politicians because it was a visible act in favor of farmers; it could be used as political patronage for obtaining support from the rice millers, the principal agents for procurement. Since the funds for the price support program were obtained from an independent source of revenue, export premiums, they were outside the control of the general budgetary process. Both the export premium, administered by the Ministry of Commerce, and the price support program, administered by the Ministry of Agriculture, were outside the parliamentary control of the regular budgetary process. Therefore, the ministries had considerable autonomy outside the control exercised by the Ministry of Finance.

The price support programs in Thailand since 1975 have lacked continuity in method and organization, and they have fluctuated in size. Typically, the volume of paddy procured was large whenever parliamentary democracy was the operating mode of government. There would be pressure for the government to embark on a support program a few months before or almost at harvest time for the wet-season crop. If in that year the government was serious about implementing the program, then the support price, the method of support, and the funding would be decided by the government around this time.

Because of the government's desire to spread the program as widely as possible, the funds available for procurement operations had to be turned over many times; this could only be done by releasing or selling rice in the market as quickly as it was purchased. To the extent that any effective withdrawal from the market through procurement operations took place, it was mainly used to fill the government-to-government order for exports. But these orders could have been filled as easily through purchases from the free market without any need to engage in costly support operations at the farm level (World Bank 1992).

Both the MOF and the PWO were small and unprepared for the administrative burden required for this task. Their ineffectiveness was aggravated as they became the major conduits for the distribution of political patronage, and the top positions in these organizations were frequently occupied by political appointees. After 1984, the administration of the program passed to the Ministry of Interior, which received a revolving fund of 200 million baht or about US$8 million. After 1984, it also became in effect a way of buying off farmers' protests. When there were signs of trouble, the Ministry of Interior went out to extinguish the flames by paying off the local leadership, usually the rice millers.

It was only in the context of the bureaucratic power and political patronage system that the paradox of taxing farmers through export taxes and export premiums, on the one hand, and providing rice support to farmers through the procurement program, on the other hand, could be explained. A logical alternative to the price support program might have been to lower export premiums at harvest time, which would have helped prevent a price decline.

Starting in 1984, the government initiated a program for subsidizing rice exports. This was, however, an indirect subsidy provided by making credit available to the exporters at subsidized rates of interest. The amount available was extremely limited; only some exporters benefited, and the rates enjoyed by the exporters were not passed on to the farmers. At the margin, the government policy did not succeed in driving the desired wedge between the domestic and border prices. The consumption subsidy program also came to an end in the mid-1980s. By the early 1990s, the price policy of the government effectively moved toward free trade so that the variation in domestic prices followed variations in world prices.

Conclusions

The experience of the Asian countries covered in the study emphasizes that in order to be effective and successful, public intervention to achieve price stabilization, with the help of public stocks and reliance on foreign trade, has to meet a few essential conditions.

1. The buffer stock agency must have assured and flexible access to financial resources, since its financial requirements cannot be predicted in advance, for example, at the beginning of the financial year. The assurance of access—not so much the actual use of financial resources—needs to be unrelated to the variability of domestic supplies, seasonal or interval.
2. The buffer stock agency must be able to regulate its timing of purchases and sales in order to influence decisions by traders and

producers. Delays in or inappropriate timing of purchases and sales would detract from its ability to influence market prices in the desired time period. Delays in purchases led to public agency buying from traders, millers, or large farmers, who could hold stocks so that the majority of the farmers ended up selling at much below procurement prices to the millers or graders. Adequate information, market intelligence, or forecasts of domestic supplies and prices are essential. Since there are no futures markets, the government has to provide crop forecasts and price information to enable the market to function effectively. The Indonesian food agency was remarkable for its success in getting information on supplies and prices prevailing in various local markets spread throughout the country. It was also efficient in processing information quickly to provide guidance for market intervention, thus reducing unanticipated lags and leads in responding to movements in supplies and prices. The managerial efficiency and technical competence of the public agency also must be of a high order. The opportunities for corruption are considerable and can greatly aggravate the adverse consequences of inefficiency.

3. The management of public stocks requires expertise not only in making cost-effective purchases and sales, but also in rolling over stocks to avoid spoilage from long-term storage. In a closed economy, rolling over a large amount of stocks may destabilize the domestic market if sales and purchases are required at times not warranted by considerations of price stability. The buffer stock agency could use the mechanism of foreign trade to roll over stocks, so long as the amount is small and it has easy access to the world market to dispose of temporary surpluses, to be replenished by purchases later on.

4. Adequacy, timeliness, and efficiency of market operations by the public agency are also required to prevent counterspeculation by private traders. At times of surplus, the traders will refrain from buying if they have no confidence in the public agency's performance; they will wait until prices fall further. Similarly, in times of shortage, private traders will buy rather than sell, with a view to making a profit from a future rise in prices. If public stocks are believed to be very low, sales from the public agency may be bought and held by private traders against a further rise in future prices, thus failing to moderate the price rise.

5. If public stock reduces or substitutes for private storage, the success of the public effort is compromised. Public stocks may provide competition to private traders if the latter are few and not competitive; this may help reduce monopolistic rents earned by private traders. In most cases, however, public storage costs are higher than private costs. The difference between ceiling and floor prices should be large enough to encourage private trade. Narrowing the price band by reducing the participation of private trade in stock operations places a larger burden on public stocks and increases the budgetary costs. Also, it requires subsidies to the public agency to cover its costs.

6. The actual operating costs of price stabilization incurred by the buffer stock agencies were often not known, since they performed other functions or undertook other income-earning activities unrelated to price stabilization policy. The sources of financing for different operations were not specified. Unless transparency was achieved in the allocation of costs relating to the multiplicity of responsibilities, it was not possible to evaluate the specific costs of price stabilization. Moreover, in a few cases, related objectives such as provision of supplies to the designated consumers imposed an inflexible burden on the agency to obtain supplies through procurement, even when domestic supplies were short or imports were not allowed, thus aggravating the price rise. Similarly, purchases were terminated when enough had been bought to meet the requirements of the public distribution system, even though surpluses in the market persisted and prices were depressed.

8

Impact of Stabilization Policy on Price Variability over Time and across Countries

What were the long-run trends of domestic prices in the different countries? How did these compare with the long-run trend in world prices? What were the magnitudes of price variability in the countries? How was price variability affected by the policies adopted? How did policies change over time in each country?

The analysis of foodgrain price instability needs to be placed in the context of the long-run trends in the prices of foodgrains in these countries. The trade and exchange rate regimes, including export and import policies, in the countries influenced both the variability of domestic prices and their long-run movements in relation to the world or border prices. Import and export policies, through their impact on net trade—the flow of exports and imports—affected the domestic supplies of foodgrains and hence year-to-year price variations. The forces that shaped the long-run trend in domestic prices also had an effect on the variability of prices. Technological changes and transformation in agriculture affected the seasonal pattern of production, including cropping intensity (the number of crops grown in a year) and their seasonal variability; they also influenced year-to-year variations in production. With technological progress in agriculture, weather-related variations in production assumed decreasing importance. Water supply became more stable through irrigation, but reliance on purchased inputs such as fertilizer increased. Moreover, the long-run trend in domestic prices was also a function of the long-run balance between supply and demand for foodgrains. As countries reached self-sufficiency, price variability became more a function of variability in domestic production than of import supplies and prices. This was especially true when they were marginally self-sufficient or imported in some years and exported in others.

As for the long-run trend in domestic prices, the real wholesale price of rice declined over time in Bangladesh, the Philippines, and Thailand, but not in Indonesia and Pakistan. There was an upward trend in Indonesia and in Basmati rice, the major export variety, in Pakistan; there was no discernible trend in IRRI rice in Pakistan. In the long run, the trend of the wholesale price of wheat was declining in Pakistan and Bangladesh.

Figure 2—Annual real wholesale price and linear trend of real border price of rice in Bangladesh, 1972/73–1990/91

Price (taka/metric ton)

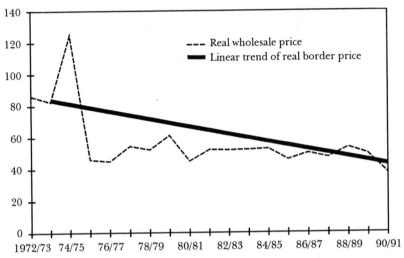

Sources: Chowdhury and Shahabuddin 1992, Tables 1 and 5.2; Bangladesh, Bureau of Statistics 1991; Goletti 1992; and Goletti 1994.

How did the real border prices of the respective foodgrains behave over time? Did the long-run trend in real wholesale prices follow the long-run trend in border prices in all countries?[12] In most cases, the long-run trends were not strong (Figures 2 to 8). The long-run trends in both the border and wholesale prices of rice were downward only in Bangladesh and Thailand; in Pakistan, the trends in both the border and wholesale prices of Basmati rice were upward. In the Philippines, the border price went up and the wholesale price went down. In Indonesia, as well, the trend in the border price was downward, whereas the trend in the wholesale price was upward. In wheat, a major crop in Pakistan, the trend in the border price was upward, the reverse of the wholesale price. In Bangladesh, the trends were downward in both the wholesale and border prices of wheat.

While "world" prices of rice and wheat (as defined by the export prices of Thai rice and U.S. wheat) had declined over the years, the "border" prices (estimated as c.i.f or f.o.b. prices) in different countries behaved differently from the world prices so defined. It was, however,

---

[12]The real domestic price is the nominal price deflated by the consumer price index (I_d) or the national income deflator where the former is not available; the real border price is the border price deflated by the combined index of unit value of manufactured goods in five major industrial countries (I_w), and the real exchange rate is the nominal exchange rate deflated by (I_w/I_d).

Figure 3—Annual real wholesale price and linear trend of real border price of rice in Indonesia, 1970–90

Price (rupiahs/kilogram)

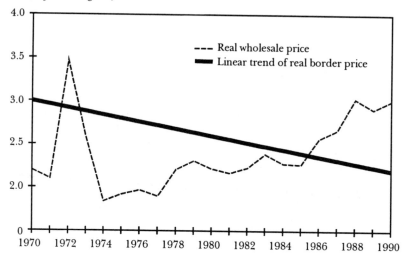

Sources: Sudaryanto, Hermanto, and Pasandran 1992; Indonesia, Central Bureau of Statistics 1988, 1992, and 1993.

Figure 4—Annual real wholesale price and linear trend of real border price of Basmati rice in Pakistan, 1963/64–1989/90

Price (rupees/metric ton)

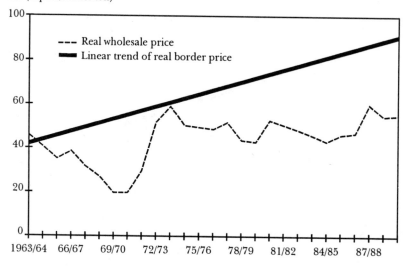

Sources: Pakistan, Finance Division 1992; United Nations, various years; and Pakistan, Ministry of Food, Agriculture, and Cooperation 1992.

Figure 5—Annual real wholesale price and linear trend of real border price of rice in the Philippines, 1960–90

Price (pesos/kilogram)

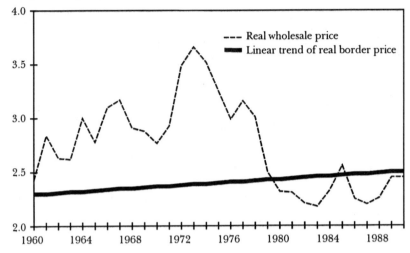

Sources: Balisacan, Clarette, and Cortez 1992; Philippines, Department of Agriculture 1992 (obtained through correspondence); United Nations, various years.

Figure 6—Annual real wholesale price and linear trend of real border price in Thailand, 1960–90

Price (bahts/metric ton)

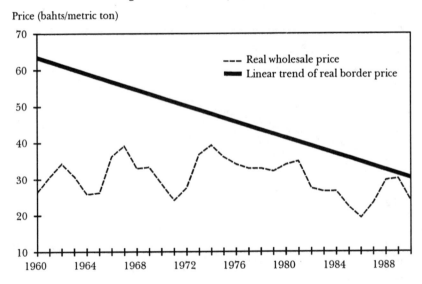

Sources: Siamwalla and Setboonsarng 1989; Siamwalla et al. 1992.

87

Figure 7—Annual real wholesale price and linear trend of real border price of wheat in Bangladesh, 1972/73–1989/90

Price (taka/metric ton)

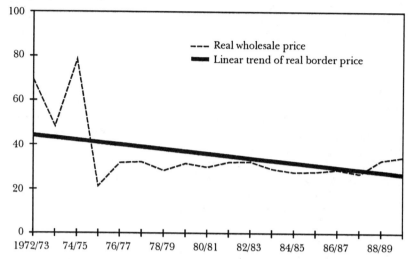

Sources: Chowdhury and Shahabuddin 1992, Tables 1 and 5.2; Bangladesh, Bureau of Statistics 1991; Goletti 1992; and Goletti 1994.

Figure 8—Annual real wholesale price and linear trend of real border price of wheat in Pakistan, 1961/62–1988/89

Price (rupees/metric ton)

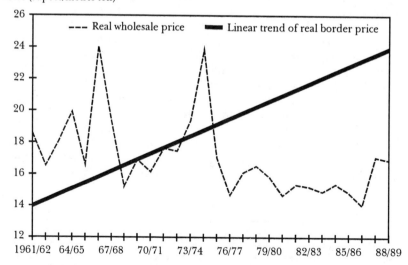

Sources: Pakistan, Finance Division 1992; United Nations, various years; and Pakistan, Ministry of Food, Agriculture, and Cooperation 1992.

the border price, the c.i.f. price of imports, and the f.o.b. price of exports that were relevant to the individual countries. While the absolute differences between "world" and "border" prices in different countries can be explained by differences in costs such as international transportation and insurance, it is not clear why there should be divergent trends in movements in prices over time unless the long-run trend in transportation and related costs was significantly different from changes in world prices so as to affect the trend in border prices. This, however, does not explain why the export prices of Thai and Pakistani rice should have divergent trends, except for the differences in quality between two types of rice catering to highly differentiated markets. Also, in some of the countries, imports of rice or wheat were obtained under food aid programs, export credits, or bilateral intergovernmental trade agreements, where prices that were negotiated were different from the prices that were quoted in the world market.

The second set of questions in connection with the movement in prices (both border and wholesale) concerns whether the real domestic wholesale prices were higher or lower than the real border prices.[13] During most of the decade of the 1980s, the domestic wholesale price of rice was above the border price in all the rice-importing countries (Indonesia, Bangladesh, and the Philippines). In Bangladesh, this was true only during the mid-1980s. In the Philippines, in 7 out of 10 years, the wholesale price was higher than the border price. In Pakistan, the wholesale price of wheat was lower than the border price from the early 1970s onward; it was higher than the border price during the 1960s. For wheat in Bangladesh, the wholesale price was lower than the border price in most years, except the beginning of the 1970s and the end of the 1980s when it was higher than the border price. During the same period, in the rice-exporting countries, Pakistan and Thailand, the wholesale prices were lower than the border prices. However, for the exporting countries, this was true in the 1960s and 1970s as well.

There was no systematic pattern over time in the way in which the wholesale price of rice moved in relation to its border price, as shown by a comparison of three-year moving averages. In the case of rice in the import-substituting countries, Bangladesh, the Philippines, and Indonesia, it was only during the 1980s, in the aftermath of domestic price policy reforms, that the domestic wholesale price moved above the border price, as indicated by the three-year moving average of prices. However, in the earlier period, before the 1970s, the wholesale prices remained in most years below the border prices except in the Philippines. In the Philippines, during the 1960s, the wholesale price was above the border price. In countries where rice was an export commod-

---

[13]A comparison between wholesale and border prices faces several shortcomings. First, there are substantial price differences among different varieties of rice or wheat, and it is not easy to ensure that prices refer to varieties of comparable quality. Second, since farmers sell their crops mostly during harvest time, comparison of annual average prices may not be a true indicator of farm-level incentives.

ity, the domestic wholesale price was consistently below the border price. In the case of wheat, which was an import-substituting commodity in Pakistan and Bangladesh, wholesale prices remained below the border price in most of the years, as indicated by the three-year moving averages of wheat prices.

The year-to-year variability of the wholesale price in the three import-substituting countries was, in general, lower during the 1980s than the 1970s. This was true for wheat in Pakistan and rice in the Philippines, Indonesia, and Bangladesh (Table 9). A significant reduction took place in rice price variability in the Philippines and Bangladesh. However, during the last two decades, there was no consistent decline between five-year periods. For example, there was an increase in variability during 1986–90 in all countries except the Philippines, compared with 1981–85; in some cases—wheat in Pakistan and rice in Bangladesh and Indonesia—the increase was significant, although the magnitude of variability was still lower than it was during the 1970s. In countries for which data for the 1960s were available, there was an increase in variability during the early 1970s compared with the late 1960s.

In Thailand, the wholesale price fluctuated the least during the late 1970s, considering the whole period from the 1960s to 1990. Variability rose significantly during the 1980s compared with the late 1970s. In Pakistan, the degree of rice price variability declined significantly during the late 1970s and early 1980s compared with the 1960s and early 1970s; as in Thailand, rice price variability went up again during the second half of the 1980s.

It is plausible to argue that the degree of instability in domestic prices in different countries may be related to, among other factors, the variability of domestic production, the relative importance of public procurement and distribution of foodgrains, and the compensating variations in stocks and imports (Table 9).[14] It is important to remember that the public interventions in the marketing and pricing of rice and wheat were not directed specifically toward minimizing variance; rather, they were directed toward implementing floor and ceiling prices, which were usually determined annually and changed from year to year, especially the floor price. The implementation of floor prices through public procurement was not always successful, one may recall, in the sense of the wholesale price rising up to the level of the procurement price.

The variability of production of rice in Bangladesh, the Philippines, and Indonesia declined during the 1980s. The decline in the variability of wheat production was significant in Bangladesh but not in Pakistan

---

[14]On the basis of a simple statistical analysis, no systematic relationship in a quantitative sense could be obtained between intercountry variations in price instability and the factors mentioned above. Without a more comprehensive analysis in individual countries and a better specification of variables, the search for such a quantitative relationship is likely to be unproductive.

between the 1970s and the 1980s. The decline in production variability was mainly due to considerable expansion of irrigation, which supplemented the water supply, offsetting the variations in rainfall. It also enabled farmers to grow three crops a year, leading to a significant expansion in winter rice cultivation. With three rice crops in a year, the probability that a shortfall in one crop would be offset by compensating variations in another crop was higher. The reduced variability was also evident in the seasonal prices. As a result of increased cropping intensity, wheat and rice harvests and hence market arrivals were distributed more evenly during the year. Also, improved transportation infrastructure, better integration of markets, an increase in the stock-output ratio, increased competition in the domestic foodgrain trade, and an increase in private-sector storage have all contributed to the reduction in seasonal price variations in recent years (UNDP 1988; Chowdhury 1989). As different regional markets became more integrated, drastic price declines in surplus areas during harvesting seasons were avoided.

In Indonesia, during the 1970s and 1980s, production variability for rice on the whole was less than that in Thailand, the Philippines, and Pakistan but was roughly comparable to that in Bangladesh. Price variability in Indonesia was in general lower than in these countries from the mid-1970s onward. This may partly be due to a higher ratio of procurement to production as well as better timing and effectiveness in Indonesia. It is noteworthy that, in Pakistan, the ratio of procurement to production was much higher than in Indonesia. This in itself is not important since it was not always designed to affect the variability of domestic price. Public procurement of rice in Pakistan, on a monopoly basis and at a low price, was designed to ensure an adequate supply of exports. Since the primary objective was very different, there was not much variability in the ratio of procurement to production. For wheat in Pakistan and rice in Indonesia, procurement was designed to affect the variability of the wholesale price. Variations in the ratio of procurement to production between different five-year periods seemed to follow interperiod changes in the variability of the wholesale prices. For example, as the ratio of procurement to production of wheat increased over time in Pakistan, the variability of the wholesale price declined. Similarly, as the ratio of procurement to production of rice increased in Indonesia between five-year periods from 1971 to 1985, the variability of the wholesale price declined. As the ratio of procurement to production declined in 1981–85, price variability increased.

However, there was no consistent pattern of relationship between the intercountry differences in the ratio of procurement to output, on the one hand, and the intercountry differences in price variability, on the other. The way in which the procurement operations were managed in terms of flexibility and timeliness—factors mentioned earlier—was crucial to the final outcome regarding the impact of procurement on price variability. It is difficult to tell from these comparisons how much procurement is needed to impart greater stability to prices. For example, the procurement ratio during the 1980s in Indonesia was higher than in the Philippines and production variability in Indonesia was also lower. In the first five-year period, price variability was lower and in the second period, price variability was higher than in the Philippines, but not much higher. This confirms to some extent expectations regarding the impact of both production variability and variability in the procurement ratio on price variability. But during the late 1970s, even this weak relationship between price variability and other factors did not exist: the procurement ratio was much higher in the Philippines, while production variability was almost the same as that in Indonesia, but price variability was much lower in Indonesia. Again, in the early 1970s, in the Philippines, the procurement ratio was lower and production variability was higher. Even then, price variability was much lower than in Indonesia. Comparing Indonesia with Bangladesh, however, the procurement ratio was consistently higher in the former than in the latter, and production variability was either equal to or slightly lower than that in Bangladesh. Price variability in Indonesia, in fact, was consistently lower than in Bangladesh, often substantially lower.

In Pakistan, the procurement ratio for rice was consistently several times higher than in any other country, and production variability during the 1980s was higher but not significantly so than in Bangladesh. However, price variability was lower in Pakistan than in Bangladesh during the 1970s but roughly the same as that in Bangladesh during the 1980s. Also, although Pakistan had a much higher ratio of procurement than the Philippines, the rice price varied more than that of the Philippines during the 1980s. In the 1970s, production variability was roughly about the same as the Philippines'. In fact, in one five-year period, production variability in the Philippines was much higher. The procurement of rice in Pakistan, it should be recalled, was heavily oriented toward export sales, and the domestic market was a residual market; one-third to one-half of total output was exported from the mid-1970s to the end of the 1980s. The variability of the wheat price in Pakistan was, on the whole, lower than in Bangladesh, but there was a smaller production variability even with a much higher procurement ratio. The case of wheat in Bangladesh was unique in that the ratio of public distribution to total consumption—70 to 90 percent—was very high. But procurement in Bangladesh was meant entirely for public distribution, and imports added to the wheat distributed. The domestic market (outside the public distribution system) was a residual market.

How did year-to-year variations in domestic prices behave in relation to the long-run trend of border prices? Did the policies succeed in stabilizing prices around the long-run trend of border prices (Figures 2 to 8)? A comparison of annual wholesale real prices with the long-run trend in real border prices shows that there was no consistent pattern for the entire time period. Only in Pakistan for wheat and only during the early years, ending in 1975/76, did the wholesale price of wheat fluctuate above and below the trend in the real border price. After 1976, fluctuations in the wholesale price were consistently below the border price. In other countries, for long periods, the fluctuations in domestic wholesale prices were either below or above the border prices—more frequently below than above. For example, the annual fluctuations in domestic prices of rice took place below the trend level of real border prices in Thailand throughout the period 1970–90, in the Philippines from 1979 onward, in Indonesia throughout the final period except for 1988–90, in Bangladesh between 1975 and 1988, and in Pakistan between 1963 and 1990 for Basmati rice and between 1975 and 1988 for IRRI rice. The fluctuations of the domestic wholesale price of rice took place above the trend level of the border price in the Philippines between 1960 and 1979, in Pakistan between 1960 and 1963 for Basmati rice, and in Bangladesh between 1970 and 1975. After 1988, in Bangladesh, the domestic price tended to fluctuate above and below the border price. In the case of wheat in Bangladesh, fluctuations took place below the trend level of the border price for the major part of the period, 1975–88; in only a few years were the movements in domestic price above the border price.

Did these countries achieve a degree of stability of domestic prices greater than that in border prices (Tables 10, 11, and 12)? If they had eliminated trade restrictions that were reinforced by interventions in domestic markets, the price fluctuations in domestic wholesale prices would have coincided with fluctuations in border prices. It appears from Tables 10, 11, and 12 that in all countries and in most cases, variability of domestic prices was lower than variations in border prices. In Indonesia and the Philippines, during the 1980s, variability of domestic prices was never higher than 56 percent of the variability of border prices; for rice in Indonesia, Bangladesh, and the Philippines during 1981–85, for example, the variability of domestic prices was as low as one-fifth to one-fourth of the variability of border prices. In Pakistan, variability of the wholesale price of wheat during 1981–85 was only one-tenth of that of the border price. In Indonesia, consistently over the two decades, the variability of domestic prices was substantially less than that of the border prices.

Regarding export crops, Thailand achieved a considerable reduction in the variability of domestic prices, compared with the variability of border prices, except during the late 1980s when interventions in domestic markets were substantially reduced. Also, it should be noted that Thailand achieved a high degree of stability in domestic prices without resorting to public stocks. In Pakistan, the objective of market interventions in rice was focused more on the level of the domestic price rather than its variability; no consistent relationship between the variations in domestic prices of rice vis-à-vis border (export) prices was expected. In fact, there were years when the variability of domestic prices was higher than that of border prices, especially during the 1980s. The objective in Pakistan was to ensure a high and more stable export price in specialized markets where Pakistan's rice was not highly competitive with Thai rice because of substantial differences in quality, grade, and taste.

Questions have been raised about the extent to which the desire to stabilize real domestic food prices explains the variations in the degree of nominal protection, that is, variations in domestic prices in relation to world prices. Could it have been the intention of the countries to raise or lower the real domestic price from one period to another or from one year to another to influence the degree of nominal protection, either positively or negatively?

Table 10—Intercountry comparison of real wholesale and border price variability of rice

Period	Philippines[a]		Thailand[b]		Indonesia[b]		Pakistan (Basmati)[c]		Pakistan (IRRI)[c]		Bangladesh[b]	
	Wholesale	Border	Wholesale	Border	Wholesale	Border	Wholesale	Border	Wholesale	Border	Wholesale	Border
1960–65	0.05	0.22	0.09	0.06	n.a.	n.a.	0.19	n.a.	n.a.	n.a.	n.a.	n.a.
1966–70	0.04	0.06	0.10	0.14	n.a.	n.a.	0.18	0.10	n.a.	n.a.	n.a.	n.a.
1971–75	0.10	0.56	0.19	0.56	0.26	0.66	0.21	0.36	n.a.	n.a.	0.38	0.23
1976–80	0.12	0.18	0.02	0.12	0.06	0.23	0.09	0.20	0.09	0.11	0.12	0.12
1981–85	0.06	0.23	0.13	0.20	0.03	0.14	0.06	0.03	0.04	0.07	0.04	0.17
1986–90	0.05	0.09	0.15	0.14	0.06	0.15	0.09	0.07	0.11	0.06	0.09	0.09

Sources: Balisacan, Clarette, and Cortez 1992; Bangladesh Bureau of Statistics 1991; Chowdhury and Shahabuddin 1992; Pakistan, Finance Division 1992; Sianwalla et al. 1992; and Sudaryanto, Hermanto, and Pasandran 1992.

Note: n.a. is "not available."

[a]For the Philippines, the border price of rice is the import parity price.

[b]For Thailand, Indonesia, and Bangladesh, the border price of rice is the c.i.f. price.

[c]For Pakistan, the border price for Basmati and IRRI rice is the export parity price.

Table 11—Intercountry comparison of real wholesale and border price variability of wheat

Period	Pakistan[a] Wholesale	Border	Bangladesh[b] Wholesale	Border
1960–65	0.06	0.09	n.a.	n.a.
1966–70	0.16	0.07	n.a.	n.a.
1971–75	0.05	0.45	0.47	0.16
1976–80	0.05	0.06	0.04	0.15
1981–85	0.01	0.10	0.02	0.05
1986–90	0.09	0.09	0.20	0.17

Sources: Balisacan, Clarette, and Cortez 1992; Bangladesh Bureau of Statistics 1991; Chowdhury and Shahabuddin 1992; Pakistan, Finance Division 1992; Siamwalla et al. 1992; and Sudaryanto, Hermanto, and Pasandran 1992.
Note: n.a. is "not available."
[a]For Pakistan, the border price for wheat is the import parity price.
[b]For Bangladesh, the border price for wheat is the c.i.f. price.

The degree of nominal protection in this context is measured by the ratio of the domestic price to the border price, converted into domestic currency at the current exchange rate. Price stabilization policy results in stability of the domestic price vis-à-vis the border price; therefore, with a stable domestic price but a falling border price, farmers are protected from the effects of the lower price. When the border price is rising, a stable domestic price protects consumers and penalizes farmers. Therefore, a policy of price stabilization allows the degree of protection to change in response to a policy to reduce the variability of the domestic price rather than to a policy or an action by the government to fix the domestic price at a level designed to protect either farmers or consumers. The hypothesis can be tested, following Timmer (1993), by an analysis of variance designed to explain the difference each year between the domestic price and the border price for the same commodity.

Table 12—Intercountry comparison of the ratio of wholesale and border price variability, 1960–90

Period	Philippines Rice	Thailand Rice	Indonesia Rice	Pakistan Basmati Rice	Wheat	Bangladesh Rice	Wheat
1960–65	0.23	1.50	n.a.	n.a.	0.67	n.a.	n.a.
1966–70	0.67	0.71	n.a.	1.80	2.29	n.a.	n.a.
1971–75	0.18	0.34	0.39	0.58	0.11	1.65	2.94
1976–80	0.67	0.17	0.26	0.45	0.83	1.00	0.27
1981–85	0.26	0.65	0.21	2.00	0.10	0.24	0.40
1986–90	0.56	1.07	0.40	1.29	1.00	1.00	1.18

Sources: Balisacan, Clarette, and Cortez 1992; Bangladesh Bureau of Statistics 1991; Chowdhury and Shahabuddin 1992; Pakistan, Finance Division 1992; Siamwalla et al. 1992; and Sudaryanto, Hermanto, and Pasandran 1992.
Note: n.a. is "not available."

The nominal protection coefficient (*NPC*) can be defined as

$$NPC = \frac{P_d}{P_w \times XR},$$

(7)

where

P_d = nominal domestic price,
P_w = nominal border price, and
XR = the official exchange rate (the amount of domestic currency per unit of foreign currency.

Further, if I_d is defined as the consumer price index in the country and I_w as the index of the unit value of manufactured goods in industrialized countries, then *NPC* can be rewritten as

$$NPC = \frac{P_d}{P_w \times XR} = \frac{P_d \times \dfrac{I_d}{I_d}}{\dfrac{P_w \times I_w}{I_w} \times XR}.$$

(8)

If rP_d is defined as the real domestic price, rP_w as the real border price, and rXR as the real exchange rate, then they can be expressed as

$$rP_d = \frac{P_d}{I_d}, \quad rP_w = \frac{P_w}{I_w}, \quad rXR = \frac{XR \times I_w}{I_d}.$$

(9)

Substituting (9) in (8) gives

$$NPC = \frac{rP_d}{rP_w \times rXR}.$$

(10)

Taking the logarithm of equation (10) gives

$$\log NPC = \log rP_d - \log rP_w - \log rXR.$$

(11)

From equation (11), it is evident that the nominal protection rate (either positive or negative) varies for three independent reasons: changes in the real domestic price, in the real world price, and in the real exchange rate.

The debate over the nominal protection rate is concerned with rP_d—changes in the real domestic price. Even if rP_d is unchanged over time, changes in the nominal protection rate can occur due to changes in the real exchange rate and in the real border price. The policy to stabilize the real domestic price is basically an attempt to isolate the real domestic price from variations in these external factors, that is, changes in rXR and rP_w. Thus, a significant change can occur in the measure of protection (NPC) even if the actual policy objective is to stabilize rP_d and not to protect the domestic producers or consumers. The NPC is the ex-post outcome of policy actions. It does not necessarily reflect the intention of the policymakers to achieve a certain degree of divergence between the domestic and border prices.

The results of the analysis of variance, which decomposes variations in the NPC into relative contributions from each of the three variables that indicate the impact of stabilization (rXR and rP_w and the protection policy, rP_d), are presented in Table 13, which shows the percentage contribution of individual or paired independent variables to the explanation of the variations in the logarithm of the NPC. Table 14 shows the same relationship in terms of first differences, changes in the NPC and other variables from one year to the next. It is evident from these tables that the contribution of year-to-year variations in domestic real prices to the year-to-year variations in NPC is rather modest. The highest contribution—only 36 percent—is in Thailand, and the lowest—3.2 percent—is in Pakistan. In terms of first differences in NPC, the greatest contribution is in the Philippines, 20 percent, and the next highest is in Indonesia, 15 percent. In all cases, however, both in logarithms of NPC and first differences, the contribution of the real border price (rP_w) and the real exchange rate (rXR) combined is the highest. This general pattern is true for wheat in Pakistan, as well as rice in Pakistan and Bangladesh. The exception seems to be wheat in Bangladesh; even this is less of an exception if first differences in the variable are considered.

Table 13—Variance analysis indicating the percentage contribution of three independent variables to variations in the nominal protection coefficient (NPC) for rice and wheat

Independent Variable	Explanation of Variations in Logarithm of NPC				
	Philippines	Thailand	Indonesia	Pakistan	Bangladesh
	(percent)				
Rice					
rPd	4.49	36.30	5.56	3.16	16.63
rPw	27.35	85.40	74.73	26.72	16.10
rXR	26.63	26.60	11.84	15.94	6.50
rPd, rPw	24.34	91.10	25.40	69.58	24.16
rPd, rXR	26.67	49.10	4.05	50.63	36.99
rPw, rXR	80.95	85.90	79.77	79.63	74.40
Wheat					
rPd	. . .	. . .	. . .	3.09	16.33
rPw	. . .	. . .	. . .	86.67	22.60
rXR	. . .	. . .	. . .	75.60	2.38
rPd, rPw	. . .	. . .	. . .	88.14	92.85
rPd, rXR	. . .	. . .	. . .	80.43	39.27
rPw, rXR	. . .	. . .	. . .	92.22	29.39

Source: Authors' calculations.
Notes: All variables are in logarithmic form. rPd = real domestic price; rPw = real border price; rXR = real exchange rate. The ellipses indicate "not applicable."

Table 14—Variance analysis indicating the percentage contribution of first differences of independent variables to variations in first differences in the nominal protection coefficient (NPC) for rice and wheat

Independent Variable	Explanation of Variations in Logarithms of NPC				
	Philippines	Thailand	Indonesia	Pakistan	Bangladesh
			(percent)		
Rice					
rPd	20.49	0.50	14.98	1.79	3.87
rPw	46.39	37.15	76.50	2.14	7.35
rXR	9.24	. . .	0.15	0.40	16.02
rPd, rPw	78.52	54.10	82.60	47.90	70.48
rPd, rXR	26.00	0.50	18.10	2.37	46.03
rPw, rXR	86.52	71.10	80.90	74.20	75.12
Wheat					
rPd	. . .	. . .	. . .	5.49	23.87
rPw	. . .	. . .	. . .	41.88	26.88
rXR	. . .	. . .	. . .	10.10	15.89
rPd, rPw	. . .	. . .	. . .	10.18	60.89
rPd, rXR	. . .	. . .	. . .	14.53	42.95
rPw, rXR	. . .	. . .	. . .	56.12	55.96

Source: Authors' calculations.
Notes: All variables are in logarithmic form. rPd = real domestic price; rPw = real border price; rXR = real exchange rate. The ellipses indicate "not applicable."

The real domestic price helps explain the changes in nominal protection. The *NPC* fluctuated below and above 1 in all countries, indicating that there was no consistent pattern of nominal protection in any of the countries except Thailand, an exporting country, where the domestic price was below the border price (implying negative nominal protection) except in the late 1980s, when domestic prices converged with border prices. In Pakistan, where rice was an export commodity, this was also the case except for two years out of the whole period. In the Philippines, the years with the highest real domestic prices, 1972–74, were the years with the lowest *NPC*. Similarly, in Pakistan, an extremely high *NPC* during the late 1960s was associated with low real domestic prices. In Bangladesh, the *NPC* during the 1980s fluctuated within a narrow range while the domestic price fluctuated significantly. In the case of wheat in Bangladesh, domestic prices fluctuated within a very narrow range, since most wheat sales took place through the public distribution system at predetermined prices during most of the 1970s and 1980s. However, the *NPC* fluctuated considerably, and in most cases, the variations in *NPC* were due to fluctuations in the border price and the rate of exchange, which in combination determined the domestic price of imports. Thus, in all countries, the movements in domestic prices relative to world prices are mainly the result of efforts to stabilize the real domestic price rather than an overt effort on the part of policymakers to affect the degree of protection for the farmers.

9

Some Quantitative Estimates of the Benefits of Stabilization

An attempt is made in this chapter to estimate the benefits from foodgrain price stabilization, following the methodology introduced by Newbery and Stiglitz (1981) and Kanbur (1984) and applied by Bautista and Gonzales (1992) to specific nonfood crops in the Philippines and by Braverman et al. (1992) to foodcrops in Brazil.

The methodology for estimating producers' benefits can be briefly stated. Suppose the producer has an income Y_0 with a mean $\overline{Y}_0$ and a coefficient of variation of σ_{Y_0}. After price stabilization, the level of income changes to Y_1, with a mean of $\overline{Y}_1$ and a coefficient of variation of σ_{Y_1}. If the benefit from price stabilization to the producer is B, that is $Y_1 - Y_0 = B$, then

$$E\,U\,(Y_0) = E\,U\,(Y_1 - B), \tag{12}$$

where U is the indirect utility function of income and E is the expectation operator. Taking a Taylor series expansion of equation (12) around the mean values and rearranging gives the following equation:

$$\frac{B}{\overline{Y}_0} = \frac{\overline{\Delta Y}}{\overline{Y}_0} - \frac{1}{2} \times R\,[\sigma_{Y_1}^2 - \sigma_{Y_0}^2], \tag{13}$$

where

$$\overline{\Delta Y} = \overline{Y}_1 - \overline{Y}_0 \tag{14}$$

is the change in the mean income before and after stabilization and R is the coefficient of relative risk aversion. Here, $B/\overline{Y}_0$ is an approximation of the estimated benefits of the scheme to producers as a fraction of their initial average income. The first term on the right-hand side, the transfer benefits, is the change in the average income as a fraction of initial income.

The second term, the risk benefits, is determined by two factors—the degree of risk aversion and the extent of reduction in income variability as a consequence of price stabilization. Thus, the total benefit is equal to the sum of the transfer and risk benefits. The transfer benefits represent the distributional impact of the program; producers may gain (or lose) at the expense of consumers or conversely. The risk benefits represent the gains (or losses) resulting from the increased (or decreased) efficiency as a result of price stabilization. The producers' income subsequent to price stabilization is the product of the new average output and the new average price. In the short run, production does not respond to changes in prices. But in the long run, output responds to the new price regime resulting from price stabilization. Output also responds to changes in the average price as well as to the variability of prices. Where prices are completely stabilized in the new price regime, there is no variability of price but only a new average price.

In the following estimation of producers' benefits, partial—not complete—stabilization is considered. Hence, there will be a change after partial stabilization in the mean price as well as in the variability of price. In actual estimation, however, even though long-run benefits are considered, response of supply or output to changes in the variability of price is not quantified. This is because all the available studies on supply response do not estimate the response of the coefficient of supply to changes in variability. Since there is no basis for assuming an approximate magnitude of elasticity of the coefficient of supply response to changes in price variability, no such coefficient could be used in the simulation study. This is indeed a limitation of the exercise. It is generally believed that output responds positively to a reduction in variability of price; hence partial price stabilization is supposed to stimulate supply.

Following Newbery and Stiglitz (1981) and Kanbur (1984), the benefits of price stabilization to consumers as a percentage of their total expenditure can also be quantified. The cash value to consumers of stabilizing the price of commodity 1 is assumed to be B, assuming all other prices to be fixed both before and after price stabilization. If income (Y) is assumed to be random,

$$E\,U\,(p_1,p_2,\cdots p_n,Y) = E\,U\,(\hat{p}_1,p_2,\cdots p_n,Y-B), \tag{15}$$

where $\hat{p}_1$ is the level at which the price of good 1 is stabilized. If $\bar{p}_1$ and $\bar{Y}_1$ are the means of p_1 and Y_1, then expanding both sides by using Taylor series expansion around the mean $\bar{p}_1$ and $\bar{Y}_1$, after eliminating various intermediate steps following Kanbur (1984), gives

$$\frac{B}{X} = \frac{1}{2}\,(1-\varepsilon)^2\,\sigma_p^2 + \left\{\frac{1}{2}\varepsilon\,\sigma_p^2\right\} - R\,\rho\,(p,Y)\,\sigma_y\,\sigma_p, \tag{16}$$

where B is consumers' benefits, X is total consumer expenditure, ε is the price elasticity of demand, σ_p is the coefficient of variation of p, R is the coefficient of risk aversion, ρ is the correlation coefficient, and σ_y is the coefficient of variation of y. The first term on the right-hand side is consumer transfer benefits. The second term is arbitrage benefits, which would occur even if the consumer is risk neutral ($R = 0$). These are pure social gains due to private storage, which remain unexploited because of imperfect markets. But, for actual values of elasticities and the coefficient of variation of prices, the arbitrage benefits are likely to be small. The benefits are further reduced if the costs of operating a buffer stock are taken into account. The last term is risk benefits, which occur as a result of reductions in price and income variability.

Quantification of consumers' benefits requires data on a wider range of variables than producers' benefits. Data are required not only on consumers' expenditures in each country, but also on consumers' income from all sources, the share of foodgrain (rice or wheat expenditure) in total income, and hence the impact of food price variation on consumers' income via the income elasticity of demand. Moreover, the formula for the quantification of benefits is based not only on the assumption of complete stabilization, but also on constant output, whereas in practice, partial stabilization and variation in output are more relevant.

The following quantitative estimates of benefits from price stabilization of rice in selected countries is based on single market analysis. The assumptions made for the different parameters are as follows:

1.	Elasticity of Demand	Elasticity of Supply
Bangladesh	−0.56	0.20
Indonesia	−0.50	0.12
Pakistan	−0.70	0.60
Philippines	−0.15	0.25
Thailand	−0.40	0.25

2. Coefficients of relative risk aversion, R = 1.0, 1.5, and 0.5 (simulation exercises were undertaken for three different levels of risks).

3. For countries where the producers' prices are not available, the wholesale price has been reduced by 20 percent to adjust for the margins.

4. Producers' revenue equals the value of crop output, which is computed as the producer price multiplied by the quantity produced (which is estimated for alternative policy regimes using output price elasticity values).

5. For producers, benefits are estimated on the basis of producers' revenue.

Three scenarios are compared in this analysis. In the historical case, various price intervention policies affect producer and consumer prices. This scenario is compared with the free trade scenario in which domestic prices are linked to the border prices (c.i.f. price or f.o.b. price, as the case may be) and with the price band scheme, in which prices are allowed to fluctuate 12 percent around the long-term border prices (linear trend). For Pakistan, the Philippines, and Thailand, a price band scheme of 8 percent around the trend has also been estimated.

Historical Case

Of the five countries studied, the variability of rice production ranges from 4 percent in Bangladesh to 11 percent in Pakistan; the variability of consumption goes from 4 percent in Bangladesh to 14 percent in

Thailand. Regarding prices, the variability of producer and consumer prices is nearly the same within the individual countries; however, intercountry differences in the variability of producer and consumer prices are wide; the variability of real producer prices ranges from 8 percent in Indonesia to 23 percent in Bangladesh, while that of the real consumer price varies from 9 percent in Indonesia to 34 percent in Bangladesh.

Instability in supply, demand, and prices causes instability in producers' revenue and consumers' surplus, as shown in Table 15. The variability of producers' revenue ranges from 12 percent in Indonesia to 21 percent in Thailand, while that of the consumers' surplus ranges from 14 percent in Pakistan to 43 percent in Indonesia.

Free Trade

Free trade is simulated by assuming that the producer and consumer prices are equal to the border price. In all five countries, the average real producer prices are higher under free trade than under the historical case. The same holds true for real consumer prices, except in Bangladesh, where they are roughly the same, and in the Philippines, where free trade consumer prices are lower than historical prices (Table 15). The real producer and consumer prices vary more under free trade than historically, fluctuating from 29 percent in Pakistan to 56 percent in Bangladesh. Compared with the historical case, the producer revenue and consumer surplus are higher in the free trade scenario, but they are more unstable than in the historical case.

The benefits resulting from a hypothetical change from the historical policy to the alternative policy of free trade and the band scheme are estimated on the assumption of different coefficients of relative risk aversion equal alternatively to 1.5, 1.0, and 0.5. They are presented in Table 16. In almost every case, removal of interventions (free trade) results in large transfer benefits to producers; under the assumption of a risk aversion of 0.5, the estimates range from 54 percent of average producer income in Thailand to 162 percent in Pakistan, which more than compensates for the negative risk premium. The total net benefits to producers range from 52 percent in Thailand to 160 percent in Pakistan. These estimates of benefits are not compared with the costs of stabilization, such as storage and interest costs, in the absence of data on comparable estimates of costs incurred in stabilization policies. Under certain assumptions, the storage costs as a percent of the total average government expenditure range from 4 percent in Bangladesh to less than 1 percent in the Philippines.

Price Band Scheme

In the price band scheme, upper and lower limits are imposed on the reference price. The upper limit is 12 percent above the reference price, while the lower limit is 12 percent below the reference price. The reference price is the long-term trend of the border price.

Table 15—Summary of the single market analysis for rice

Item	Historical Policy	Free Trade Policy	Band Scheme
Bangladesh			
Producer revenue			
Mean (million Tk)	458,764.38	1,013,795.30	1,035,227.00
Variability (percent)	20	34	21
Producer surplus			
Mean (million Tk)	112,036.20	362,380.00	423,041.20
Variability (percent)	12	23	21
Consumer surplus			
Mean (million Tk)	834,600.50	943,494.00	791,587.10
Variability (percent)	21	41	37
Producer price			
Mean (Tk/metric ton)	34.15	83.15	81.30
Variability (percent)	23	56	41
Consumer price			
Mean (Tk/metric ton)	83.66	83.15	81.20
Variability (percent)	34	56	41
Production			
Mean (1,000 metric tons)	13,684.00	13,786.15	13,700.01
Variability (percent)	4	11	11
Consumption			
Mean (1,000 metric tons)	13,985.67	13,786.15	13,721.20
Variability (percent)	4	11	11
Indonesia			
Producer revenue			
Mean (million Rp)	27,255.17	54,316.52	54,792.05
Variability (percent)	12	31	23
Producer surplus			
Mean (million Rp)	8,911.34	21,622.10	21,001.30
Variability (percent)	4	8	5
Consumer surplus			
Mean (million Rp)	51,076.13	64,306.95	63,327.66
Variability (percent)	43	46	44
Producer price			
Mean (1,000 Rp/metric ton)	1.21	2.60	2.59
Variability (percent)	8	40	27
Consumer price			
Mean (1,000 Rp/metric ton)	2.17	2.60	2.59
Variability (percent)	9	40	27
Production			
Mean (1,000 metric tons)	21,094.77	27,481.66	21,507.81
Variability (percent)	5	5	5
Consumption			
Mean (1,000 metric tons)	22,893.27	21,481.66	23,328.87
Variability (percent)	6	5	4
Pakistan			
Producer revenue			
Mean (million Rs)	74,389.16	194,652.02	192,800.23
Variability (percent)	16	33	29
Producer surplus			
Mean (million Rs)	36,213.80	59,908.10	111,381.30
Variability (percent)	24	26	21
Consumer surplus			
Mean (million Rs)	11,398.90	19,438.40	12,891.30
Variability (percent)	14	19	17
Producer price			
Mean (Rs/metric ton)	28.03	68.20	69.30
Variability (percent)	22	29	28

(continued)

Table 15—Continued

Item	Historical Policy	Free Trade Policy	Band Scheme
Consumer price			
Mean (Rs/metric ton)	35.03	68.20	69.30
Variability (percent)	12	29	28
Production			
Mean (1,000 metric tons)	2,651.69	2,986.10	2,681.10
Variability (percent)	11	13	11
Consumption			
Mean (1,000 metric tons)	1,834.84	2,702.62	1,900.04
Variability (percent)	15	13	11
Philippines			
Producer revenue			
Mean (million P)	5,877.32	10,368.94	10,397.54
Variability (percent)	14	37	30
Producer surplus			
Mean (million P)	3,150.60	6,311.60	6,200.20
Variability (percent)	31	38	40
Consumer surplus			
Mean (million P)	47,899.40	35,681.90	39,983.30
Variability (percent)	17	38	39
Producer price			
Mean (P/metric ton)	1.47	2.48	2.30
Variability (percent)	13	35	32
Consumer price			
Mean (P/metric ton)	3.14	2.48	2.30
Variability (percent)	13	35	32
Production			
Mean (1,000 metric tons)	4,201.58	4,261.67	4,252.98
Variability (percent)	6	26	28
Consumption			
Mean (1,000 metric tons)	4,434.82	4,261.67	4,338.79
Variability (percent)	6	26	28
Thailand			
Producer revenue			
Mean (million B)	468,136.21	718,762.90	701,670.80
Variability (percent)	21	31	26
Producer surplus			
Mean (million B)	86,754.90	137,687.30	131,223.40
Variability (percent)	12	18	16
Consumer surplus			
Mean (million B)	83,800.02	108,440.20	110,600.30
Variability (percent)	31	40	40
Producer price			
Mean (B/metric ton)	30.56	46.90	47.40
Variability (percent)	15	33	31
Consumer price			
Mean (B/metric ton)	36.68	46.90	47.40
Variability (percent)	16	33	31
Production			
Mean (1,000 metric tons)	15,318.10	15,518.68	15,422.00
Variability (percent)	9	21	20
Consumption			
Mean (1,000 metric tons)	12,771.36	15,518.68	13,168.30
Variability (percent)	14	20	16

Source: Authors' calculations.
Note: A 12 percent band is used around the long-run trend of the border price.

Table 16—Simulation results of producer benefits for rice, based on single market analysis, using a 12 percent band

	R = 0.5		R = 1.0		R = 1.5	
Item	Free Trade Policy	Band Scheme	Free Trade Policy	Band Scheme	Free Trade Policy	Band Scheme
Bangladesh						
Transfer	120.9839	125.6555	120.9839	125.6555	120.9839	125.6555
Risk	−1.8900	−0.1025	−3.7800	−0.2050	−5.6700	−0.3075
Net benefits	119.0939	125.5530	117.2039	125.4505	115.3139	125.3480
Indonesia						
Transfer	99.2889	101.0336	99.2889	101.0336	99.2889	101.0336
Risk	−2.0425	−0.9625	−4.0850	−1.9250	−6.1275	−2.8875
Net benefits	97.2464	100.0711	95.2039	99.1086	93.1614	98.1461
Pakistan						
Transfer	161.6672	159.1779	161.6672	159.1779	161.6672	159.1779
Risk	−2.0825	−1.4625	−4.1650	−2.9250	−6.2475	−4.3875
Net benefits	159.5847	157.7154	157.5022	156.2529	155.4197	154.7904
Philippines						
Transfer	76.4229	76.9095	76.4229	76.9095	76.4229	76.9095
Risk	−2.9325	−1.7600	−5.8650	−3.5200	−8.7975	−5.2800
Net benefits	73.4904	75.1495	70.55793	73.3895	67.6254	71.62954
Thailand						
Transfer	53.5371	49.8860	53.5371	49.8860	53.5371	49.8860
Risk	−1.3000	−0.5875	−2.6000	−1.1750	−3.9000	−1.7625
Net benefits	52.2371	49.2985	50.9371	48.7110	49.6371	48.1235

Source: Authors' calculations.
Notes: The band scheme denotes a 12 percent band around the long-run trend of the border price. R is the coefficient of risk aversion. Producers' benefits under free trade and the band scheme are expressed as a percentage increase over producers' benefits in the historical case.

In all five countries the real producer and consumer prices are more stable under the band scheme than under free trade (Table 15). This is significantly so in Bangladesh and Indonesia and less so in the other countries. The producer and consumer prices, however, are more stable under the historical case than under the band scheme. The average prices under the band scheme are not significantly different from the free trade prices, but the variability is lower. Under the band scheme, producer revenue is less variable than under free trade, but more variable than in the historical case, except in Bangladesh, where variability of producer revenue is about the same in the historical case and under the band scheme. The positive transfer benefits to producers are significantly larger than the negative risk benefits, resulting in positive net benefits. The net benefits range from 49 percent of the average producer's revenue in Thailand to 158 percent in Pakistan. However, the net benefits for the producers under the band scheme are higher than those under the free trade policy, except in Thailand and Pakistan, where they are slightly less than free trade.

In summary,

1. The band scheme reduces price variability below that in free trade, but not below the historical case.
2. The transfer benefits to producers are large compared with the negative risk benefits. The free trade situation or the band scheme brings net total benefits to producers, compared with the historical case. For most countries, the producers' benefits are larger under the price band scheme than under free trade, except in Thailand and Pakistan. The large increase in benefits under free trade, compared with those under the historical case, is because the mean or average price under free trade is higher than that under historical policy.
3. The increase in the producers' benefits under price stabilization with a band over what is achieved under free trade is quite small, varying from 10 percent to less than 3 percent. The highest increase in benefits (expressed as a ratio of producers' benefits to average producers' revenue) is 10 percent for Bangladesh with a relative risk aversion of 1.5. The lowest increase in benefits under a risk aversion of 1.5 is 6 percent for Indonesia. However, in Pakistan and Thailand, the producers incur a loss compared with the situation under free trade, even though the loss is very small in size.
4. Under the band scheme (12 percent above and below long-term trend prices), there was little reduction in price variability compared with free trade. Consequently, alternative estimates of producers' benefits were undertaken with a lower price band— 8 percent below and above the trend price rather than 12 percent (Table 17). The lower price band did reduce price variability as expected, but the reduction was significant in only three countries. With a lower price band, price variability was reduced from 31 percent to 25 percent in Thailand, from 32 percent to 28 percent in the Philippines, and from 28 percent to 23 percent in Pakistan. The benefits for producers, with risk aversion at 0.5, increased in only one case from 52 percent to 63 percent in Thailand. They decreased from 160 percent to 156 percent in Pakistan, and from 74 percent to 71 percent in the Philippines.

In estimating the benefits of price stabilization, to what extent does the degree of risk aversion affect the benefits? In other words, the higher the degree of risk aversion, the greater should be the benefits from price stabilization. When producers' benefits were estimated assuming degrees of risk aversion varying from 0.5 to 1.5, the higher the degree of risk aversion, the higher the benefit of price stabilization in relation to the free trade situation. For example, in Bangladesh, the producers' benefits under the price band are 5 percent higher than under free trade with a risk aversion ratio of 0.5, whereas they are higher than those under free trade by 7 percent with a risk aversion ratio of 1.0 and 8 percent with a ratio of 1.5.

Table 17—Simulation results of producer benefits for rice, based on single market analysis, using an 8 percent band

Item	R = 0.5		R = 1.0		R = 1.5	
	Free Trade Policy	Band Scheme	Free Trade Policy	Band Scheme	Free Trade Policy	Band Scheme
Pakistan						
Transfer	161.6672	156.8661	161.6672	156.8661	161.6672	156.8661
Risk	−2.0825	−1.0500	−4.1650	−2.1000	−6.2475	−3.1500
Net benefits	159.5847	155.8161	157.5022	154.7661	155.4197	153.7161
Philippines						
Transfer	76.4229	72.3534	76.4229	72.3534	76.4229	72.3534
Risk	−2.9325	−1.4700	−5.8650	−2.9400	−8.7975	−4.4100
Net benefits	73.4904	70.8834	70.5579	69.4134	67.6254	67.9434
Thailand						
Transfer	53.5371	63.3633	53.5371	63.2087	53.5371	63.2087
Risk	−1.3000	−0.3375	−2.6000	−0.6750	−3.9000	−1.0125
Net benefits	52.2371	63.0258	50.9371	62.5337	49.6371	62.1962

Source: Authors' calculations.
Notes: The band scheme denotes an 8 percent band around the long-run trend of the border price. R is the coefficient of risk aversion. Producers' benefits under free trade and the band scheme are expressed as a percentage increase over producers' benefits in the historical case.

How do the estimates change if instead of current rates of exchange, the equilibrium rates of exchange are used? For illustrative purposes, this exercise is undertaken for only two countries, Bangladesh and the Philippines, where estimates of equilibrium rates of exchange are available (Tables 18 and 19).

The free trade and band scheme alternatives are compared with the historical situation. Since the historical case is governed by both prevailing exchange rates and interventions for price stabilization, the free trade and band scheme scenarios are re-estimated with equilibrium rates of exchange. Under the equilibrium exchange rate scenario, the variability of prices (consumer and producer) is lower than that under the prevailing exchange rate; in the Philippines it is lower by 6 percent and in Bangladesh it is significantly lower—20 percent. Also, the variability of producers' revenue is 30 percent lower in Bangladesh and 16 percent lower in the Philippines, and the variability of consumers' surplus is 10 percent lower in both countries. As a result, the reduction in price variability under the band scheme is less significant than under the free trade situation, especially in Bangladesh.

Under the equilibrium exchange rate scenario, producers receive more benefits with free trade and the band scheme than with the prevailing exchange rates. In Bangladesh, producers' benefits are 20 to 25 percent higher and in the Philippines, 40 percent higher.

The previous analysis of benefits from price stabilization referred to rice, the principal cereal in most of the countries included in the study.

Table 18—Summary of the single market analysis for rice, using an equilibrium exchange rate, Bangladesh and the Philippines

Item	Historical Policy	Free Trade Policy	Band Scheme
Philippines			
Producer revenue			
Mean (million P)	5,877.32	13,455.65	12,111.32
Variability (percent)	14	31	28
Producer surplus			
Mean (million P)	3,150.60	6,606.01	6,345.98
Variability (percent)	31	32	26
Consumer surplus			
Mean (million P)	47,899.40	35,702.11	36,702.10
Variability (percent)	17	34	31
Producer price			
Mean (P/kilogram)	1.47	2.51	2.54
Variability (percent)	13	33	30
Consumer price			
Mean (P/kilogram)	3.14	2.51	2.54
Variability (percent)	13	33	30
Production			
Mean (1,000 metric tons)	4,201.58	4,301.51	4,376.12
Variability (percent)	6	24	27
Consumption			
Mean (1,000 metric tons)	4,434.82	4,301.51	4,440.23
Variability (percent)	6	24	26
Bangladesh			
Producer revenue			
Mean (million Tk)	458,764.38	1,273,112.00	1,154,963.40
Variability (percent)	20	24	21
Producer surplus			
Mean (million Tk)	112,036.20	361,134.00	419,862.20
Variability (percent)	12	23	21
Consumer surplus			
Mean (million Tk)	834,600.50	932,861.00	774,884.50
Variability (percent)	21	37	33
Producer price			
Mean (Tk/metric ton)	34.15	84.12	83.80
Variability (percent)	23	48	41
Consumer price			
Mean (Tk/metric ton)	83.66	84.12	83.80
Variability (percent)	34	48	41
Production			
Mean (1,000 metric tons)	13,684.00	13,900.15	13,654.50
Variability (percent)	4	11	10
Consumption			
Mean (1,000 metric tons)	13,985.67	13,655.00	13,722.20
Variability (percent)	4	11	11

Source: Authors' calculations.

Notes: The band scheme denotes a 12 percent band around the long-run trend of the border price. Producers' benefits under free trade and the band scheme are expressed as a percentage increase over producers' benefits in the historical case.

Table 19—Simulation results of producer benefits for rice, using an equilibrium exchange rate

Item	R = 0.5		R = 1.0		R = 1.5	
	Free Trade Policy	Band Scheme	Free Trade Policy	Band Scheme	Free Trade Policy	Band Scheme
Philippines						
Transfer	177.5089	151.7552	177.5089	151.7552	177.5089	151.7552
Risk	−0.4400	−0.1025	−0.8800	−0.2050	−1.3200	−0.3075
Net benefits	177.0689	151.6527	176.6289	151.5502	176.1889	151.4477
Bangladesh						
Transfer	128.9419	106.0688	128.9419	106.0688	129.1291	106.0688
Risk	−2.9325	−1.3325	−3.825	−2.665	−5.7375	−3.9975
Net benefits	126.0094	104.7363	125.1169	103.4038	123.3916	102.0713

Source: Authors' calculations.
Notes: The band scheme denotes a 12 percent band around the long-run trend of the border price. R is the coefficient of risk aversion. Producers' benefits under free trade and the band scheme are expressed as a percentage increase over producers' benefits in the historical case.

In Pakistan, however, wheat is the predominant cereal and has been subject to serious efforts to stabilize prices. In Bangladesh, wheat is secondary to rice in the urban and semi-urban areas. Hence, separate estimates of benefits are provided for wheat (Tables 20 and 21). Historically, the variability of the producer price and producers' revenue in Pakistan was less than half of that in Bangladesh. In Pakistan, the variability of the producer price was higher than that of the consumer price. Under free trade policy in Pakistan, the variability of the producer price more than doubled, and that of the consumer price increased three times. Under the price band scheme, the variability of both the producer and consumer prices was less than that under free trade but more than in the historical case. The benefits from price stabilization for wheat were higher than for free trade, even though in absolute terms it was only about 24 percent of the producers' income. With a higher degree of risk aversion, as expected, the benefits of price stabilization increase relative to those of free trade. For rice, on the other hand, the benefits from stabilization were lower than under free trade mainly because the average revenue from stabilization was less than under free trade, even though price variability was slightly less. For wheat, price stabilization resulted in a higher average producers' revenue than free trade.

For wheat in Bangladesh, free trade, compared with the historical case, led to a decline in the average producers' revenue. With price stabilization, however, the average producers' revenue increased not only more than under free trade but also more than under the historical case, leading to an increase in producers' benefits. Moreover, it was the only case for all of the countries where price variability under a price stabilization policy was significantly lower than under either the historical case, or free trade. As a result, producers' benefits under free trade

Table 20—Summary of the single market analysis for wheat

Item	Historical Policy	Free Trade Policy	Band Scheme
Bangladesh			
Producer revenue			
Mean (million Tk)	26,619.08	24,607.94	27,897.36
Variability (percent)	26	17	23
Producer price			
Mean (Tk/kilogram)	35.21	34.97	36.62
Variability (percent)	29	14	11
Production			
Mean (million metric tons)	741.06	701.23	763.66
Variability (percent)	23	19	13
Pakistan			
Producer revenue			
Mean (million Rs)	147,390.03	174,607.94	183,696.62
Variability (percent)	14	29	23
Consumer surplus			
Mean (million Rs)	19,867.41	16,783.92	14,418.62
Variability (percent)	12	21	19
Producer price			
Mean (Rs/kilogram)	17.19	19.14	19.98
Variability (percent)	12	28	19
Consumer price			
Mean (Rs/kilogram)	18.31	19.14	19.98
Variability (percent)	9	28	19
Production			
Mean (1,000 metric tons)	8,577.37	9,138.21	9,211.68
Variability (percent)	8	11	7
Consumption			
Mean (1,000 metric tons)	9,486.30	8,922.67	8,852.66
Variability (percent)	9	10	7

Source: Authors' calculations.
Note: The band scheme denotes a 12 percent band around the long-run trend of the border price. Producers' benefits under free trade and the band scheme are expressed as a percentage increase over producers' benefits in the historical case.

were negative, whereas those under the band scheme were positive and almost equal to the negative benefits under free trade.

The foregoing discussion of the benefits of food price stabilization does not distinguish between various groups of producers and consumers or between rural farm and urban nonfarm populations. These different groups of producers and consumers have different consumption patterns of foodgrains as well as different income and price elasticities of demand. For example, a study by Tyers and Anderson (1992) distinguishes between farmers, workers, and owners of industrial capital. The risk aversion ratio is assumed to be 2.0 in a developing country for all types of consumers and producers. Farmers are assumed to consume 50 percent of the total available foodgrains (say, rice), 67 percent from their own output and 33 percent from imports. Domestic prices vary in response to variations in domestic production as well as in imports. However, in an open economy, variations in domestic production are reflected in variations in imports, and prices are determined by

Table 21—Simulation results of producer benefits for wheat

| | R = 0.5 | | R = 1.0 | | R = 1.5 | |
| | Free Trade | Band | Free Trade | Band | Free Trade | Band |
Item	Policy	Scheme	Policy	Scheme	Policy	Scheme
Bangladesh						
Transfer	−7.5553	4.8021	−7.5553	4.8021	−7.5553	4.8021
Risk	0.9675	1.2675	1.9350	2.5350	2.9025	3.8025
Net benefits	−6.5878	6.0696	−5.6203	7.3371	−4.6528	8.6046
Pakistan						
Transfer	18.4666	24.6330	18.4666	24.6330	18.4666	24.6330
Risk	−1.6125	−0.8325	−3.2250	−1.6650	−4.8375	−2.4975
Net benefits	16.8541	23.8005	15.2416	22.9680	13.6291	22.1355

Source: Authors' calculations.
Notes: The band scheme denotes a 12 percent band around the long-run trend of the
border price. R is the coefficient of risk aversion. Producers' benefits under free
trade and the band scheme in all tables are expressed as a percentage increase
over producers' benefits in the historical case.

import prices. Farmers spend 50 percent, workers 20 percent, and
owners of industrial capital about 7 percent of their incomes on
foodgrains. Twenty-five percent of national income accrues to farmers,
62 percent to workers, and 13 percent to owners of industrial capital.
The price and income elasticities of demand of farmers for foodgrains
equal 0.5, whereas those of workers equal 0.1. The coefficient of variation of production is 10 percent and that of the border price is
20 percent.

The total benefits to the different classes of a reduction in the
variability of price by 50 percent (that is, the reduction in the variability
of the border price in the domestic market from 20 percent to 10 percent) are as follows. The counterfactual scenario against which the
benefits of price stabilization are estimated is one in which the worker's
wages are adjusted to compensate for a change in food price, while price
variability is 20 percent. The owners of industrial capital vary the wage
bill as food prices change. The benefits as a percentage of average
income of various groups are

Farmers	0.20
Workers	−0.05
Industrial owners	2.70

Farmers are comparatively indifferent to a reduction in price variability because they consume a large proportion of their own output.
They are, therefore, affected both as consumers and as producers. Their
gains as producers are partly offset by losses due to relatively inelastic
price demand for foodgrains. The nonagricultural workers are also
indifferent to food price changes under the assumption made here,
because they are compensated by wage indexation or payments in kind

to offset food price variations. This has the effect of annulling the benefits of price stabilization to risk-averse workers.

The major benefits accrue to the owners of industrial capital because payments to labor dominate value-added in the nonagriculture sector. Fluctuations in these payments made by the owners result in substantial profit risk. Therefore, the gains to the owners of industrial capital far outweigh the gains to farmers or workers. The former are a relatively influential group in developing countries. If they must bear the burden of price fluctuations, they exert pressure on the government to stabilize food prices. If no adjustment is made for food price changes, then the urban classes (workers and the owners of capital) share the costs of instability and hence the benefits of stabilization.

The available data do not permit the estimation or quantification of the cost of price stabilization policies in the countries under study. For one thing, the relevant public-sector agency performs multiple functions besides price stabilization or "buffer stock operations" per se; in many countries, they are engaged in providing subsidized food to designated consumers and also distributing food below cost or free in some cases for employment generation or feeding programs. Available country studies do not provide a detailed breakdown of costs and revenues to enable even an approximate analysis of the costs of different functions of the public-sector agencies. On the basis of fragmentary data, it appears that most food agencies required and received either direct or indirect subsidies and were not self-financing. Direct subsidies were either in the form of cash subsidies or free food aid received from international donors. In Bangladesh in 1989/90, the subsidy amounted to 30 percent of the purchase cost of food (the purchase cost does not include free food aid; revenues include all sales of food aid but not freely distributed food). The total subsidy amounted to 20 percent of total current public expenditure in 1989/90 (Ahmed, Chowdhury, and Ahmed 1993).[15]

In Pakistan, the subsidy on wheat procurement and distribution amounted to 45 percent of public-sector current expenditures during the late 1980s and early 1990s (World Bank 1994). In the Philippines, even without marketing, storage, and distribution costs, the difference between the purchase price and the sales price of rice involved a subsidy of 8 percent to the purchase cost; the percentage of subsidy would be several times higher if the costs of transportation and storage were included (Dawe and Timmer 1991). In Indonesia, where the principal means of financing the food agency was guaranteed access to flexible

---

[15]Francesco Goletti undertook an illustrative simulation exercise for Bangladesh to demonstrate how the cost of buffer stock operations would differ depending on how they were carried out. The open market operations were based on domestic procurement and foreign trade in order to minimize the variance of the rice price around a target price or to stabilize prices within a predetermined price band. These were compared with current policy, based on free food aid imports and domestic procurement, which seeks to implement a support price for producers and to distribute subsidized food to designated consumers or under various feeding and employment programs. The latter required larger stocks and involved higher costs than the other two alternatives (Goletti 1992).

credit facilities, the credit granted to the agency was 13 percent of all credit provided to all public-sector agencies and 2.5 percent of the total credit provided by the banking system to all the sectors (private and public). The aggregate expenditures undertaken by the food agency were as large as 8.4 percent of the total public expenditures on agriculture (both current and capital) (World Bank 1990).

Regarding the various components of the cost of food distribution by the public-sector agencies, it is roughly estimated that the cost of distribution and marketing (including storage and transportation costs) amounted to 22 percent of the purchase cost in 1989/90 in Bangladesh (Ahmed, Chowdhury, and Ahmed 1993), 33 percent in Pakistan in 1985/86 (Alderman, Chaudhry, and Garcia 1988), and 30 percent in Indonesia in 1988/89 (Sukriya, Sugeng, and Milyo 1989). Interest costs were an important component of the costs of distribution, varying, for example, from 40 to 44 percent in Pakistan and Indonesia.

10

Rethinking
Price Stabilization
Policy

In recent times there has been a certain amount of rethinking under way in policymaking circles regarding the desirability of achieving foodgrain price stabilization and the optimum method of public intervention.

Over the last two decades in Thailand and Indonesia, rapid growth in per capita income has been accompanied by a decline in the share of the principal cereal—rice or wheat—in total consumption and the role of foodgrains as a source of rural income. These countries have also experienced a significant reduction in both urban and rural poverty. As a consequence, the adverse impact of fluctuations in food prices on consumers' and producers' welfare, except for the poorest groups, is no longer as important as it was in the past. At the same time, agricultural output and rural income are being diversified in several countries in response to changes in domestic demand, comparative costs, and external trade possibilities of agricultural commodities, including cereal crops. At least in high-income developing countries in Asia, these developments have stimulated a reappraisal of the role of price stabilization and the cost-effectiveness of the ways in which this objective is pursued by governments.

As the farming sector becomes richer and more organized, the political influence of agricultural producers may increase, as happened in the past in Japan and Korea. Over time this may create pressure for higher incomes or prices for cereal producers. As income disparity between rural and urban areas widens with rapid industrialization, leading to urbanization, the pressure to maintain rural incomes may increase.

There is a general trend toward privatization and liberalization of the input and output markets in developing countries, resulting partly from their own past experience of unsatisfactory performance of the public sector and the shortcomings of extensive government regulation of the market. This trend is partly influenced by the experience of other regions and changes in the climate of opinion in the world outside, which affect the relative roles of the public and private sectors. The process of increased emphasis on market liberalization and deregulation has been accelerated under the various structural adjustment or economic policy reform programs, implemented under the aegis of and financed by the international donor community. Comprehensive policy reforms for the liberalization of the trade and foreign exchange regime have also proceeded at a rapid pace, strengthened partly by the Uruguay Round trade agreement.

In reconsidering the methods used for food price stabilization, policymakers are searching for noninterventionist and market-oriented measures. Faced with scarcity of public financial resources and the need to reduce fiscal deficits, public expenditures are being thoroughly examined for ways to use resources economically and efficiently. It is increasingly recognized that comprehensive policy reforms are likely in the short run to affect the poor adversely; the forces of growth will increase employment and income levels of the poor only in the medium and long runs. To protect the poor against the adverse effects of economic adjustment and reform, they must be protected against rises in food prices, which can adversely affect their consumption and nutrition. It is in this context that ways to devise and implement cost-effective food subsidies targeted to the poor are being reexamined.

As has already been described, significant changes have taken place or are under way in several of the countries included in this report. Thailand made the most significant change when it abolished export taxes on rice. The small price support program, oriented mainly toward traders and rice millers rather than farmers, serves primarily as an instrument of political patronage to party supporters. Its effectiveness is limited. Since the majority of the rural poor are small farmers who have a marketable surplus (most of the market surplus is not produced by a few big farmers but by a large number of small farmers), the policy emphasis is on raising the productivity of small farmers, expanding their incomes and employment through diversification of output. They benefit from high food prices, whereas the urban poor suffer.

Bangladesh has abolished both rural and urban public food rationing, the main components of the public food distribution system, because they were ineffective and did not reach the target groups. The release prices of the public distribution system in urban areas were raised over time to narrow the gap between "rations" and the market price, so that it gradually became unnecessary as a source of food for the poor. The rural rationing system, fraught with corruption, was subject to massive leakage and inadequate supplies. Currently, effective systems for delivering food to the poor are feeding programs (both urban and rural) and food-for-work programs (mostly rural).

Private participation in foreign trade in rice has been permitted in Bangladesh; its role in the domestic market is being strengthened by increased access to credit. There are transitional problems of adaptation and implementation, and private trade will need time to develop trade connections and outlets in world markets. It takes time to institutionalize access to credit after decades of exclusion of rice traders from bank credit. There is also the problem of inadequate private storage. Farmers hold 80 percent of stocks and traders, 20 percent. Open market operations are based on a wider margin between procurement prices and the open market sales price in order to encourage stockholding for seasonal stabilization by private traders. Public agencies are experimenting with different types or systems of procurement so that market prices determine the procurement by the public agency through competitive bidding. The idea is to provide additional market demand at times of surplus to prevent a sharp fall in prices.

Less significant changes have taken place or are under consideration in the other Asian countries. Pakistan has substantially liberalized or privatized domestic and foreign trade in rice, with abolition of the government's monopoly in export of rice as well as monopoly procurement in the domestic market. The subsidy on wheat has been progressively reduced, but the support price program for producers has continued. The gap between the support (procurement) price of wheat and its sales price has widened as the subsidy on wheat distribution has been reduced and the role of the private sector has increased.

In Indonesia, where private traders have traditionally played a more important role than in other countries, 80 percent of the peak season crop output was held by the private sector to be carried over to the lean season; if the private sector carried over the whole amount of the peak season surplus, a wider margin between seasonal prices would be necessary to make it worthwhile. Private traders argue that a part of the interseasonal stocks is held, not because seasonal price differences make it profitable, but for operational reasons such as ensuring regular supplies of paddy to the rice mills and rice to consumers. The major part of private traders' profit comes from the conversion of paddy into rice—from the margin between the paddy and rice prices (Ellis 1993b). Thus, public procurement is needed to prevent a sharp drop in prices in the peak season. If the private sector is to expand its stockholding operations further, seasonal price variations would have to grow substantially (Ellis 1993b). In recent years, the margin between the floor and the ceiling prices has been widened to promote an expanded role for private trade.

In view of the reduced importance of rice in the consumption basket of government employees—the majority of whom are, in any case, middle income or higher—the provision of food rations to "budget groups" as a salary supplement is being increasingly questioned. In recent years, the recipients of rations have often sold them in the market. Instead of supplying rations to budget groups, it is debated whether their salaries should be adjusted upward, targeting the direct provision of food rations to low-income groups alone.

On the other hand, so long as the agency holds public stocks for price support operations as well as for man-made or natural disasters, it needs to manage inventories by rolling them over or renew stocks periodically to prevent a deterioration in quality. Sales to the budget group have traditionally provided a way of rolling over stocks without destabilizing markets; otherwise unloading of stocks on to the market might be undertaken when supplies were abundant. To prevent a sharp drop in prices in the peak season, procurement operations by the public agency can be restricted to a few well-chosen regions that produce substantial surpluses in peak seasons. Private trade is expected to transmit the effects of a targeted intervention or procurement in specific localities quickly and widely to other seasons and other areas. This will reduce the size of stocks to be held by the public sector.

In the Philippines, not much change has taken place in the operations of the National Food Authority, although its high costs and relative inefficiencies in managing public stocks have been under scrutiny in recent years. Much discussion has been focused on improving the timeliness and flexibility of its procurement operations. Alternative ways of protecting poor consumers and rice producers against price fluctuations are being actively debated (Balisacan, Clarette, and Cortez 1992).

11

Conclusions

Traditional welfare analysis concludes that, in general, the micro-level economic benefits of price stabilization for both consumers and producers are small. The framework of this analysis assumes that the primary objective of the producers and consumers is to maximize utility—an unrealistic assumption for poor producers and consumers in developing countries. On the contrary, the poor in developing countries pursue the overriding objective of achieving economic security, that is, minimum subsistence income and access to basic food supplies at all times. The simulation exercises, on the basis of such restrictive assumptions and currently available estimates of risk aversion, do not yield high benefits. Moreover, this approach does not explore the macroeconomic benefits of price stabilization, including concerns for social and political stability. Much more analysis and quantification of the macroeconomic aspects of price stabilization are required. While current economic analysis continues to cast doubt on the size of the benefits to be derived from price stabilization, poor consumers, producers, and governments in all countries prefer less rather than more instability of food prices.

The governments of the five countries included in this study, like those of other developing countries, were unwilling to let seasonal or interyear fluctuations in foodgrain prices be determined entirely by national or international market forces. The socioeconomic and political consequences of a high degree of fluctuation in food prices were unacceptable. There was a consensus that both steep rises in foodgrain prices, which adversely affect poor consumers, and significant declines in prices in the postharvest season or in a particular year, which failed to provide a floor to producers' prices, were unacceptable. In the early years of the Green Revolution, governments relied heavily on the diffusion of high-yielding technology based on investment in irrigation and purchased inputs to accelerate domestic food production. Governments wanted to ensure that increased output resulting from investment did not trigger a steep fall in prices that would dash farmers' expectations of high earnings and act as a disincentive to technological progress.

The lessons of experience indicate that while fluctuations—both seasonal and interyear—were on the whole reduced by public intervention, budgetary costs of stabilization as well as the costs of overall resource misallocation were often high. The average long-run domestic prices around which fluctuations took place—admittedly lower than would have occurred without public intervention—frequently diverged from the long-run trend of world prices. This was partly, if not entirely, because price stability was only one component in a set of multiple objectives that included promotion of self-sufficiency in food, increased (or at least stable) foreign exchange earnings and government revenues, and redistribution of income to protect or enhance the real income of particular interest groups.

Four out of the five countries covered here attached high priority to the objective of food self-sufficiency. Bangladesh, Indonesia, Pakistan, and the Philippines had high and rapidly rising cereal imports during the 1960s and 1970s. Starting in the 1960s, foreign exchange constraints propelled a strong drive toward the adoption of the Green Revolution in both rice and wheat. All of the countries sought to protect their domestic markets against relatively high fluctuations in the world rice market. The world market for rice was more volatile than that for wheat: supplies and prices fluctuated more. Rice was the principal cereal consumed in Thailand, but it was also an export crop, whereas in Pakistan rice was a secondary cereal but mainly an export crop. Fluctuations in domestic production and exports in Thailand, a major exporter of rice in the world market, affected world supplies and prices. Indonesia, on the other hand, was a large importer of rice. Given the small size of the international market for rice, an increase in Indonesia's rice imports to meet domestic shortages led to a rise in import prices.

The relative importance of the different objectives changed over time and for different crops. The objective of maximizing foreign exchange and tax revenues in Thailand was not necessarily consistent with the objective of assuring incentive prices for farmers, except on the assumption that export demand was inelastic and the elasticity of domestic supply was low. More important, so long as export taxes of various kinds constituted a major source of government revenue, as in Thailand, there was a limit to the degree of flexibility with which taxes could be used to stabilize domestic price fluctuations. In Bangladesh, Indonesia, and Pakistan, the obligation to ensure adequate public food distribution meant that the amount of procurement by the public agency at harvest time was inflexible, which did not always support efforts to stabilize prices. When there were shortfalls in production, procurement had to be undertaken even when no procurement should have taken place.

The pursuit of multiple functions or divergent objectives impeded the analysis of costs and benefits of the price stabilization policy in isolation. For example, the size of public stocks required to stabilize prices was not distinguished from what was needed for food distribution to poor consumers or government employees, for meeting emergency requirements in the event of natural calamities, or for financing programs such as food-for-work programs or nutritional feeding of poor children and pregnant women.

All countries have regulated imports, exports, and public stocks to varying degrees and in different ways to achieve stabilization. The major thrust of domestic stock operations has been toward seasonal price stabilization, whereas imports have been the major instrument for inter-year price stabilization. However, there have been shortcomings in forecasting and programming the procurement of imports. Errors in forecasts and unanticipated leads and lags in exports and imports have sometimes aggravated rather than ameliorated fluctuations. Imports and exports have not been coordinated with the arrival of domestic supplies in the market. In issuing quotas and licenses to private traders in foodgrains, public sector trading agencies have delayed decisions and follow-up actions. The response of public-sector purchasing agencies or trade regulatory authorities to changes in market conditions was sluggish and subject to over- or underreaction. Experience indicates that domestic private enterprise should be allowed to operate in both foreign trade and domestic markets because private traders respond to market signals faster.

Commercial imports in several countries were supplemented by food aid. Food aid brought its own particular set of rigidities and delays in the commitment and disbursement of food supplies in response to changes in the market situation. A multiyear commitment of food aid with an option to draw on it in response to year-to-year changes in food supply could have introduced a considerable degree of flexibility. Also, it would have been helpful to allow conversion of food aid to cash aid and to allow use of aid funds to obtain food supplies from sources other than aid-giving countries to allow for more flexibility in purchasing supplies, for example, from the cheapest sources of supply or those that could respond quicker.

In a net importing country, fluctuations in prices arise from fluctuations not only in domestic production but also in import prices. Flexible access to foreign exchange resources for imports at times of domestic shortage, even at higher prices in world markets, is crucial to stabilization efforts. Foreign exchange resources should be earmarked for food imports in response to year-to-year price changes. Easy, quick access to adequate imports to meet fluctuations in domestic production can reduce domestic political pressure to achieve food self-sufficiency even at high opportunity costs. Conversely, rapid fluctuations in import prices and a limited ability to meet such fluctuations encourage the drive toward self-sufficiency at high cost.

A broader concept of stability may be desirable. Concentrating on stability in one cereal rather than a composite of cereals reduces flexibility. With a diversity of cropping and consumption patterns, more than one crop may play a crucial role in stabilizing foodgrain prices. This already is happening with wheat and rice in South Asia. Also, the price of one particular input (such as fertilizer) relative to the price of an output (rice or wheat) can play a crucial role in stabilizing producers' prices in all countries. In the countries covered in this study, variations in the price of rice or wheat, as the case may be, were frequently looked at in the context of volatility of the price of fertilizer, which was crucial for ensuring profitability of production or producers' incentives. This was particularly so in Indonesia, where the fertilizer price was explicitly linked to determination of the floor or support price for producers; it was implicitly so in Bangladesh and Pakistan. Fertilizer prices in the world market were also highly volatile, which was especially relevant for countries relying predominantly on fertilizer imports. If in a year a fall in the output price accompanied a fall in fertilizer prices, concern about the price drop was greatly diminished. However, there is no a priori reason why both prices should move together.

Experience indicates that the first step in promoting foodgrain price stabilization is to ensure that foodgrain markets function efficiently; that is, the private sector should be able to function unhindered in storing, marketing, and processing foodgrains. This includes not only traders and marketing intermediaries but also farmers who hold surplus stocks. What is necessary is to remove legal or institutional constraints on private marketing intermediaries. In some countries, government regulations restrict storage and interregional movements of foodgrains or restrict access to credit for foodgrain storage in the name of discouraging "hoarding"; the participation of private trade is often prohibited in the export and import of foodgrains. Public policy should be designed to eliminate constraints on trade and to promote access to credit and market integration to facilitate and encourage private trade to respond to price signals. In addition, it may be necessary to take positive action to promote private trade, not only through investment in infrastructure (such as roads, transportation, and communication facilities) and promotion of market intelligence, but also in some cases, in lieu of inefficient and costly public storage and marketing, it may be more efficient to provide limited public subsidies in the short run to private traders, so that over time they can gain experience and reap the economies of scale afforded by construction and maintenance of large-scale warehouses in an open economy.

The case for intervening through public stocks to stabilize prices becomes less urgent if the foodgrain is widely traded in the world market. Stabilizing prices also becomes less important as countries gain experience in using foreign trade as a stabilizing factor, as domestic markets become more integrated, and as information on the foodgrain market is improved. In some countries with changing seasonal patterns of production and technological progress, production variability and price variability have declined over time.

Countries can seek to reduce extremely wide fluctuations in food prices by smoothing out significant fluctuations around a long-term trend in the world price, so that efficiency and comparative cost considerations are not sacrificed. For example, a five-year moving average of the border price—the import or export parity price—may be used as the basis for determining the target price.[16] For a limited period, in the early stages of diffusion of new technology, the target price may be set at a level higher than the long-run average border price. This can be justified as a means of either stimulating investment in technological progress (the infant industry argument), or compensating for the limited short-run opportunities of rural income diversification, or attaining a minimum level of food self-sufficiency.

---

[16]Even the use of the long-run trend price in the domestic market, adjusted periodically in terms of five-year moving averages, would be an improvement over the current situation where target prices are not linked to long-term supply and demand considerations.

The next question is how to determine the desired range of permissible price fluctuations. From the operational point of view, minimizing fluctuations around the trend or aiming at a predetermined level of coefficient of variation in price around the trend is not a practical measure. A price band with a fixed ceiling and floor around a target price is operationally more convenient. The band should be wide—wide enough to leave adequate incentive for private traders to hold stocks and to undertake a stabilizing role. In an importing country, if the actual import parity price falls below the floor price, taxes on imports will be required. If, on the other hand, the target actual import parity price exceeds the ceiling price, subsidies on imports are in order. Similarly, in the case of a traditional exporter, taxes and subsidies will be necessary to smooth out fluctuations within a band of ceiling and floor prices around the export parity price.

However, year-to-year production fluctuations may be so wide that a country imports in one year and generates an export surplus in another, as was the case in Indonesia, for example. In an open economy without restrictions on external and internal trade, fluctuations in domestic prices take place within the range of the import and export parity price. The gap between the import and the export parity price is determined by the costs of internal marketing, distribution, and transportation; in countries with inadequate or underdeveloped marketing and distribution networks or infrastructure, the differences between the export and import parity prices are wide. The commodity, in fact, takes on the nature of a nontradable commodity. As soon as the prices move beyond the export-import parity gap, owing to fluctuations either in world prices or in domestic supply conditions, the commodity becomes tradable.

If the target ceiling and floor prices lie within the band of export and import parity prices, this would require that exports are subsidized to defend the floor price and imports are subsidized to defend the ceiling price. This would create a heavy burden on the budgetary resources of the government. If the price band (between ceiling and floor prices) is around either the export parity price or the import parity price, a combination of taxes and subsidies will be needed to maintain the price band. If, however, the price band is wide enough to lie outside the band of export and import parity prices, taxes will be used in both cases.

It follows from the foregoing that the width of the band and its relation to import and export parity prices, especially in a country that alternates between net imports and net exports are important considerations determining the financial viability of the price stabilization policy. If a price band policy is to be followed, considerable flexibility is needed in fixing annual ceiling and floor prices so that they are adjusted in accordance with movements in domestic production and in world prices. A policy of taxes and subsidies on trade with a view to stabilizing domestic prices requires the maintenance of a "buffer fund" as distinguished from buffer stock, that is, a fund of resources financed by taxes and subsidies. This is most efficiently done if the government is able to build up a stabilization fund, to which tax receipts are paid and from which subsidies are withdrawn, which can be protected from the pressing demand for resources from the rest of the government to finance general budgetary operations.

Reliance on trade policy cannot totally do away with the need for public stocks. When a country is an occasional exporter or importer of a commodity, its link with the world market is often tenuous. There is, under the circumstances, a heightened insecurity about the ability to obtain imports in years of shortfall or to dispose of export surplus in the world market. The country may need to locate buyers and impinge on the regular commercial trading arrangements of other exporting countries. Where foreign trade is conducted not by a public agency but by private traders, an additional effort needs to be made to ensure a smooth flow of trade at times of need. In many developing countries foreign trade in foodgrains has for many decades been in the hands of public-sector agencies, even when both public agencies and private traders coexist in the domestic market. It takes time for private traders to function effectively in import and export markets, following a policy of liberalization or privatization of foreign trade. It takes time to acquire experience in gathering and processing information about the world market in foodgrains, including availability, prices, and international shipping or transportation arrangements. Also, there may be occasions when surpluses or shortfalls in domestic output are substantial and, within a short time, large sales or purchases must be made. At these times, public intervention may be needed to supplement the efforts of private traders. So, even when foreign trade conducted by private traders is the principal vehicle for implementation of a price stabilization policy, the public-sector agency may need to play a residual supporting role.

There is yet one more important reason for a residual role for public stocks. There is always a time lag between making the decision to import or export and the actual arrival of the imports or disposal of the exports on the domestic markets. Domestic buffer stocks are needed to tide the country over the time lag. In view of the time lag involved in either procuring imports or undertaking exports, variations in prices cannot always be exclusively dealt with by trade policy without any recourse to public stocks. This is especially true at a time of acute and large-scale food shortage.

The diversity of circumstances facing different countries determines the relative emphasis on two policies, reliance on trade and public stocks. In many countries, there is the need for a gradual transition from a regime of heavy reliance on buffer stocks to one of reliance on trade. They need to "learn by doing" the progressive reliance on markets, both national and foreign trade, to achieve stabilization in a highly politically sensitive area of foodgrain prices. Sudden drops or rises in food prices due to domestic production fluctuation or variations in world prices continue to cause concern or worry in most developing countries. These are circumstances when domestic production fluctuations get intertwined with changes in world supply and prices. Moreover, a domestic production shortfall affects world prices when a country such as Indonesia is a large participant in the world market so that import prices go up when import needs go up.

A country may be located in an agroclimatic zone or weather pattern that affects a large number of producing and consuming countries at the same time. This is frequently the case with rice because it is a commodity that is principally produced and consumed in Asia and affected by roughly similar agroclimatic factors that cause variations in production. These factors support a residual role for some public stocks.

With improved self-sufficiency in some Asian countries as well as growth in per capita income, concern with food price fluctuations per se decreases. The impact of a sudden rise in prices on the poorest consumers is the main concern. Similarly, an unforeseen collapse in producers' prices due to an unusually large harvest is a major concern.

In most countries, a safety net program for the poorest people is increasingly being implemented. A safety net program, intended to protect the poor when food prices rise abnormally, consists of feeding vulnerable groups or subsidizing targeted food distribution or work programs with wages paid in cash or in food or a combination of these measures. These measures should be clearly distinguished from an open market operation to stabilize prices, even though they may be stabilizing under certain circumstances. Monetary payment rather than payment in food may be introduced, depending on the nutritional and consumption effects of different systems of payment. This will reduce the role of public stocks and enhance the role of private trade in the actual distribution of food to the market. Similarly, to mitigate the hardships and disincentives sustained by food producers at times of a sudden and substantial drop in producers' prices, public procurement may be undertaken to prevent a sharp drop in prices below long-run costs. However, stocks should be sold as soon as the market price goes above the floor price. Domestic procurement by a public agency may have to be combined with exports at times of abnormally low world prices, if necessary, with the help of export subsidies. The foregoing policy, which relies heavily on trade and resorts to public stock operations as a residual policy to deal with sharp rises or steep falls, would require much smaller public stocks than otherwise. In this policy framework, private trade plays a major role.

As the developing economies liberalize domestic trade and open up to international markets and price signals, and as trade restrictions and protectionist policies are abandoned following implementation of the Uruguay Round agreement, trade measures to achieve a degree of price stability would depart from the new rules of the game. Under the new trade regime, developing countries are expected not only to adopt tariffication in lieu of quantitative controls in imports, but also to "bind" tariffs at a maximum level beyond which they cannot increase them further, although they can reduce them. In practice, however, they have been given some freedom to maneuver: they are allowed to fix tariff ceilings above the currently applied rates, and the majority have fixed very high ceilings. They can continue to raise tariffs so long as the level is below the ceiling. So long as they remain below the ceiling level of bound tariffs, they may continue to use tariffs to regulate imports and import prices in order to implement domestic ceiling and floor prices. It is not clear, however, whether they can provide import subsidies, since, in principle, import subsidies are not trade-restricting but trade-promoting measures: they may provide subsidies in addition to lowering tariffs. But new export subsidies are prohibited. In fact, over time the developing countries must reduce all export subsidies in use today, with the exception of export subsidies that relate to export marketing and transport. Therefore, subsidies to compensate for the gap between high domestic prices and low export prices are not permitted.

However, countries are permitted to purchase for and sell from food security stocks at administered prices. In other words, domestic ceiling and floor prices are allowed to be implemented so long as they are not coupled with taxes and subsidies on trade, given the leeway provided by high tariff ceilings. To the extent that floor and support prices to farmers are above market prices, they are considered to be domestic subsidies. Under the Uruguay Round agreement, the aggregate measure of subsidy (resulting from different types of subsidy) should not exceed 10 percent (as against 5 percent for developed countries). Also, developing countries are allowed to undertake subsidized food distribution to meet the requirements of the urban and rural poor on a regular basis (FAO 1995c). It should be noted, however, that implementation of the trade reforms can extend up to 10 years by developing countries and 6 years by developed countries. Moreover, the experience with trade-based stabilization prices could throw up problems and challenges that developing countries can take up during the next round of negotiations on agricultural trade liberalization. In view of the limited liberalization of agricultural trade in the current round, the World Trade Organization is mandated to start new negotiations in the final year of the six-year implementation term.

A relevant question in the aftermath of the Uruguay Round agreement is what will happen to fluctuations in world food prices with trade liberalization? To the extent that protectionist policies in the past shifted the impact of fluctuations in domestic production to the world market and insulated the domestic market from external fluctuations, the elimination or reduction of protectionist policies is expected to help reduce price instability in the world market for foodgrains.[17] On the other hand, there is likely to be a reduction in world cereal stocks, especially in the developed countries, resulting from the reduction in the domestic support programs. In the past, the public stock policy for foodgrains in the principal developed, exporting countries cushioned the impact of fluctuations in world supplies caused by weather or other

---

[17]Various modeling exercises undertaken to test the trade liberalization scenarios focused more on quantifying the effects on prices than on price fluctuations. It is strange considering that one of the factors responsible for the rise of protectionism in the past was the effort to protect domestic markets from the effects of instability in the world market. One study of the impact of production fluctuations on price at the level of trade liberalization envisaged in the Uruguay Round found that liberalization would have little effect on price stability. The production shocks chosen for simulation in the model were a generalized 5 percent decline in cereal output in the year 1999 and its effect on world prices in the year 2000. Further study and research on the subject is warranted (FAO, Committee on Commodity Problems 1995a, 1995b).

natural events.[18] In the post-Uruguay Round period, a decline in the amount of stocks held in the rich, exporting countries is likely to remove this stabilizing element. In this context, a reduction in the stocks of foodgrains in developed countries below what is required to stabilize the world market may create uncertainty. There may be a need for some kind of international understanding among the major producing and exporting countries to hold the minimum amount of stocks needed to alleviate acute fluctuations in world supplies (FAO 1990).

---

[18]In the past, governments in exporting countries held stocks over and above their calculated need to ensure their reliability as suppliers. Also, food-aid donors held reserves to meet unexpected requirements. The decline in food aid flows might reduce the stock that would otherwise be available for meeting shortfalls in supplies in importing countries. Moreover, a decline in publicly held stocks due to a cutback in domestic supply programs in developed, exporting countries may not be fully compensated by a rise in private stocks (FAO 1990).

Bibliography

Ahmed, A. 1992. *Operational performance of the rural rationing program in Bangladesh*. Working Papers on Food Policy in Bangladesh No. 5. Washington, D.C.: International Food Policy Research Institute.

Ahmed, R. 1988. Food price stabilization in developing countries: Issues instruments and implementation. International Food Policy Research Institute, Washington, D.C. Mimeo.

Ahmed, R., and A. Bernard. 1989. *Rice price fluctuation and an approach to price stabilization in Bangladesh*. Research Report 72. Washington, D.C.: International Food Policy Research Institute.

Ahmed, R., N. Chowdhury, and A. Ahmed. 1993. *Determination of procurement price of rice in Bangladesh*. Working Papers on Food Policy in Bangladesh 6. Washington, D.C. International Food Policy Research Institute.

Alderman, H., M. G. Chaudhry, and M. Garcia. 1988. *Household food security in Pakistan: The ration shop system*. Working Papers on Food Subsidies 4. Washington, D.C.: International Food Policy Research Institute.

Alwang, J. 1991. *A literature review of public food distribution in Bangladesh*. Working Papers on Food Policy in Bangladesh No. 1. Washington, D.C.: International Food Policy Research Institute.

Anderson, J. R., and P. Hazell. 1989. Synthesis and needs in agricultural research and policy. In *Variability in grain yields: Implications for agricultural research and policy in developing countries*. Baltimore, Md., U.S.A.: Johns Hopkins University Press.

Arifin, B. 1992. Southeast Asian agriculture in transition: Implications for food policy. Remarks at an IFPRI seminar on Southeast Asian agriculture, September.

——. 1993. BULOG'S contribution to food security. Speech at the Non-Aligned Movement Ad Hoc Working Group on Food Security Meeting, Jakarta, February.

Asian Development Bank. 1988. *Evaluating rice market intervention policies: Some Asian examples*. Manila.

Atmaja, S., S. Amat, and M. Sidik. 1989. The role of BULOG in the Indonesian economy. *Indonesian Food Journal* 1 (1): 70–82.

Balisacan, A. M., R. L. Clarette, and A. M. Cortez. 1992. *The food problem in the Philippines: Situation, issues, and policy options*. Diliman, the Philippines: University of Philippines.

Bangladesh, Bureau of Statistics. 1991. *Statistical yearbook of Bangladesh*. Dhaka: Ministry of Planning.

Banum, L. C., R. Fabre, C. Balbosa, and E. Castro. 1992. *Food security: Performance assessment and future directions for NFA*. Manila: Development Alternatives.

Bautista, R., and C. M. Gonzales. 1992. Domestic stabilization of export crop prices: Philippine copra and Malaysian rubber. *The World Economy* 15 (November): 779–792.

Berck, P., and D. Bregman, eds. 1993. *Food security and food inventories in developing countries*. Oxford, U.K.: CAB International.

Bigman, D. 1982. *Coping with hunger: Toward a system of food security and price stabilization*. Cambridge, Mass., U.S.A.: Ballinger.

————. 1985. *Food policies and food security under instability*. Lexington, Mass., U.S.A., and Toronto, Canada: Heath.

————. 1988. Targeted subsidy programs under instability: Objectives and trade-offs. *Journal of Policy Modeling* 10 (1): 46–60.

Bigman, D. and S. Reutlinger. 1979. Food price and supply stabilization: National buffer stocks and trade policies. *American Journal of Agricultural Economics* 61 (November): 657–667.

Binswanger, H. B. 1980. Attitudes towards risks: Experimental measurement evidence in rural India. *American Journal of Agricultural Economics* 62 (August): 395–407.

Braverman, A., R. Kanbur, A. S. Brandao, and J. Hammer. 1992. Commodity price stabilization and policy reform: An approach to the evaluation of the Brazilian price band proposals. World Bank, Washington, D.C.

Braverman, A., R. Kanbur, A. S. Brandao, J. Hammer, M. R. Lopez, and A. Tan. 1990. *Costs and benefits of agricultural price stabilization in Brazil*. Policy Research Working Paper No. 564. Washington, D.C.: World Bank.

Buccola, S. T., and C. Sukume. 1991. Regulated-price and stock policies: Interaction effects and welfare preference. *Journal of Development Economics* 35 (1): 281–305.

Chowdhury, N. 1989. The changing food systems: Storage marketing and distribution issues. In *Food strategies in Bangladesh*. Bangladesh: Planning Commission.

―――. 1992. *Rice markets in Bangladesh: A study in structure, conduct, and performance*. Washington, D.C.: International Food Policy Research Institute.

Chowdhury, O. H., and Q. Shahabuddin. 1992. A study of food situation and outlook of Asia: Country report on Bangladesh. International Food Policy Research Institute, Washington, D.C.

Claessens, S., and R. C. Duncan, eds. 1993. *Managing commodity price risk in developing countries*. Baltimore, Md., U.S.A.: Johns Hopkins University Press for the World Bank.

Coady, D. 1990. Pricing policy in developing countries: The case of Pakistan. *Pakistan Journal of Applied Economics* 9 (1): 28–69.

Clarette, R. L., R. Fabre, C. Balbosa, and E. Castro. 1992. Securing food security: Performance assessment and future directions for the National Food Authority. Manila: Development Alternatives. Mimeo.

Cochrane, W. W. 1980. Some nonconformist thoughts on welfare economics and commodity stabilization policy. *American Journal of Agricultural Economics* 62: 508–511.

Dawe, D., and P. Timmer. 1991, *Rice price stabilization: Contrasting experiences in the Philippines and Indonesia*. Agricultural Policy Analysis Project II Research Report No. 339. Cambridge, Mass., U.S.A.: Harvard Institute for International Development, Harvard University.

Deaton, A. 1989. *Savings in developing countries: Theory and review*. Research Program in Development Studies Discussion Paper No. 144. Princeton, N.J., U.S.A.: Princeton University, Woodrow Wilson School.

Deaton, A., and G. Laroque. 1991. *Estimating the commodity price model*. Princeton, N.J., U.S.A.: Princeton University, Research Program in Development Studies.

―――. 1992. On the behavior of commodity prices. *Review of Economic Studies* 59 (158): 1–24.

de Janvry, A., M. Fafchamps, and E. Sadoulet. 1991. Peasant household behavior with missing markets: Some paradoxes explained. *Economic Journal* 101 (November): 1400–1417.

Diamond, P. A., and J. E. Stiglitz. 1975. Increases in risk and risk aversion. *Journal of Economic Theory* 8 (July): 337–360.

Dillon, J. L., and P. L. Scandizzo. 1978. Risk attitudes of subsistence farmers in Northeast Brazil: A sampling approach. *American Journal of Agricultural Economics* 60 (3): 425–435.

Drèze, J. H. 1974. Investment under private ownership: Optimality, equilibrium, and stability. In *Allocation under uncertainty: Equilibrium and optimality*, ed. J. Drèze. New York: Macmillan.

Ellis, F. 1989. Future rice strategy in Indonesia: Rice self-sufficiency and rice price stability. *Indonesian Food Journal* 1 (1): 27–46.

————. 1990. The rice market and its management in Indonesia. *IDS Bulletin* [Institute of Development Studies] 21 (3): 44–51.

————. 1993a. Food security and stabilization of rice prices in Indonesia. In *Food security and food inventories in developing countries*, ed. P. Berck and D. Bergman. Oxford, U.K.: CAB International.

————. 1993b. Private trade and public role in staple food marketing: The case of rice in Indonesia. *Food Policy* 18 (October): 428–438.

FAO (Food and Agriculture Organization of the United Nations). 1990. *Intergovernmental group on grains: The effects of trade liberalization on levels of cereal stocks*. 24th Session. Rome.

————. 1993. Rice policy of Pakistan: Developments in the eighties and early nineties. Rome.

————. 1995. Committee on Commodity Problems Report 95/13. 26th Session. Rome.

FAO (Food and Agriculture Organization of the United Nations), Committee on Commodity Problems. 1995a. *Impact of the Uruguay round on agriculture*. Sixth Session. Rome.

————. 1995b. *Intergovernmental group on grains: The Uruguay round final act and its implications for the world grains economy*. 26th Session. Rome.

Gardner, B. 1990. *The economics of agricultural policies*. New York: McGraw-Hill.

Ghosh, S., C. L. Gilbert, and A. Hallet. 1987. Stabilizing speculative commodity markets. Oxford: Clarendon Press.

Goletti, F. 1991. Poverty and price stabilization. International Food Policy Research Institute, Washington, D.C. Mimeo.

————. 1992. The liberalization of the public foodgrain distribution system in Bangladesh. International Food Policy Research Institute, Washington, D.C. Mimeo.

————. 1994. *The changing public role in a rice economy approaching self-sufficiency: The case of Bangladesh*. Research Report 98. Washington, D.C.: International Food Policy Research Institute.

Goletti, F., R. Ahmed, and N. Chowdhury. 1992. *Optimal stock for the public foodgrain distribution system in Bangladesh*. Working Papers on Food Policy in Bangladesh No. 4. Washington, D.C.: International Food Policy Research Institute.

Goletti, F., R. Ahmed, and N. Farid. 1995. Structural determinants of market integration: The case of rice markets in Bangladesh. *The Developing Economies* 33 (June): 185–202.

Hamid, N., I. Nabi, and A. Nasim. 1990. *Trade, exchange rate and agricultural pricing policies in Pakistan*. Washington, D.C.: World Bank.

Hazell, P. B. R. 1982. *Instability in Indian foodgrain production*. Research Report 30. Washington, D.C.: International Food Policy Research Institute.

————. 1992. The appropriate role of agricultural insurance in developing countries. *Journal of International Development* 4 (6): 567–582.

————. 1994. Potential benefits to farmers of using futures markets for managing coffee price risks in Costa Rica. International Food Policy Research Institute, Washington, D.C. Mimeo.

Hazell, P., and R. Stewart. 1993. Should Costa Rica's grain markets be liberalized? *Food Policy* 18 (December): 471–481.

Hazell, P., C. Pomerada, and A. Valdés. 1986. Epilogue. In *Crop insurance for agricultural development: Issues and experience*, eds. P. Hazell, C. Pomerada, and A. Valdés. Baltimore, Md., U.S.A.: Johns Hopkins University Press.

Helmberger, P., and R. Weaver. 1977. Welfare implications of commodity storage under uncertainty. *American Journal of Agricultural Economics* 59 (4): 639–651.

Helms, J. L. 1985. Expected consumer surplus and the welfare effects of price stabilization. *International Economic Review* 26 (3): 603–617.

Hossain, M. 1990. Natural calamities, instability in production, and food policy in Bangladesh. *Bangladesh Development Studies* 18 (4): 33–54.

Indonesia, Central Bureau of Statistics. Various years. *Statistical yearbook of Indonesia*. Jakarta, Indonesia.

Intal, P., and J. Power. 1990. *Trade, exchange rate, and agricultural pricing policies in the Philippines*. Washington, D.C.: World Bank.

Just, R. 1988. Making economic welfare analysis useful in the policy process: Implication of the public choice literature. *American Journal of Agricultural Economics* 70 (2): 448–453.

Kanbur, S. M. R. 1984. How to analyze commodity price stabilization: A review article. *Oxford Economic Papers* 36 (3): 336–358.

Kanbur, S. M. R., and D. Vines. 1984. North-South interaction and commodity control. Department of Applied Economics, Cambridge University, Cambridge, U.K. Mimeo.

Krishna, R., and A. Chhibber. 1983. *Policy modeling of a dual grain market: The case of wheat in India*. Research Report 38. Washington, D.C.: International Food Policy Research Institute.

Knudsen, O., and J. Nash. 1990. Domestic price stabilization schemes in developing countries. *Economic Development and Cultural Change* 38 (3): 539–558.

———. 1988. Agricultural price stabilization and risk reduction in developing countries. World Bank, Washington, D.C. Mimeo.

Krueger, A. O., M. Schiff, and A. Valdés, eds. 1991. *The political economy of agricultural pricing policy*, vol. 2, *Asia*. A World Bank Comparative Study. Baltimore, Md., U.S.A.: Johns Hopkins University Press.

Massell, B. F. 1969. Price stabilization and welfare. *Quarterly Journal of Economics* 83 (2): 284–298.

———. 1970. Some welfare implications of international price stabilization. *Journal of Political Economy* 78 (2): 404–417.

McKinnon, R. I. 1967. Futures markets, buffer stocks, and income stability for primary producers. *Journal of Political Economy* 75 (December): 844–861.

Miranda, M., and P. Helmberger. 1988. Effects of commodity price and stabilization programs. *American Economic Review* 78 (1): 46–58.

Moscardi, E., and A. de Janvry. 1977. Attitudes toward risk among peasants: An econometric approach. *American Journal of Agricultural Economics* 59 (4): 710–716.

Naqvi, S. N. H., and N. A. Burney. 1992. *Food situation outlook for Pakistan*. Islamabad: Pakistan Institute for Development Economics.

Newbery, D. M. 1984. Commodity price stabilization in imperfect or cartelized markets. *Econometrica* 52 (3): 563–578.

———. 1989. Theory of food price stabilization. *Economic Journal* 99 (398): 1065–1082.

Newbery, D. M., and J. E. Stiglitz. 1981. *The theory of commodity price stabilization: A study in the economics of risk*. Oxford, U.K.: Oxford University Press.

Oi, W. 1961. The desirability of price instability under price competition. *Econometrica* 29 (1): 58–64.

Osmani, S. R., and M. A. Quasem. 1990. *Pricing and subsidy policies for Bangladesh agriculture*. Research Monograph No. 11. Dhaka: Bangladesh Institute of Development Studies.

Pakistan, Finance Division. 1992. *Economic survey*. Islamabad: Finance Division.

Pakistan, Ministry of Food, Agriculture, and Cooperatives. 1988. Report of the National Commission on Agriculture. Islamabad.

———. 1991. *Agricultural statistics of Pakistan*. Islamabad.

———. 1992. *Agricultural statistics of Pakistan*. Islamabad.

Panayotou, T. 1989a. *Food price policy in Thailand*. Development Discussion Paper No. 251. Cambridge, Mass., U.S.A.: Harvard Institute for International Development, Harvard University.

———, ed. 1989b. Thailand: The experience of a food exporter. In *Food price policy in Asia*. Ithaca, N.Y., U.S.A.: Cornell University Press.

Pearson, S. P. 1990. Financing rice price stabilization in Indonesia. *Indonesia Food Journal* 4 (7): 63–83.

Peck, A. E., ed. 1977. *Selected writings on futures markets*, vol. II. Chicago, Ill., U.S.A.: Chicago Board of Trade.

Philippines, Department of Agriculture. 1990. *The Philippine agricultural development plan, 1991–1995*. Manila.

Pinckney, T. C. 1986. Stabilizing Pakistan's supply of wheat: Issues in the optimization of storage and trade policies. *The Pakistan Development Review* 25 (Winter): 451–466.

———. 1988. *Storage, trade, and price policy under production instability: Maize in Kenya*. Research Report 71. Washington, D.C.: International Food Policy Research Institute, February.

———. 1989. *The demand for public storage of wheat in Pakistan*. Research Report 77. Washington, D.C.: International Food Policy Research Institute.

———. 1991. Is market liberalization compatible with national food security? Government goals and maize policies in Southern Africa. Paper prepared for the IFPRI Conference on Market

Integration and Trade in Southern Africa, Nyanga, Zimbabwe, November 19–21.

———. 1993. Producers' price expectations and the size of the welfare gains from price stabilization. *Review of Marketing and Agricultural Economics* 51 (2): 163–197.

Pindyck, R. S. 1988. Irreversible investment, capacity choice and the value of the firm. *American Economic Review* 78 (5): 969–985.

Ravallion, M. 1987. *Markets and famines*. New York: Clarendon Press.

———. 1990. Market responses to anti-hunger policies: Effects on wages, prices and employment. In *The political economy of hunger*, ed. J. Drèze and A. Sen. Oxford: Clarendon Press.

Reutlinger, S. 1987. The pros and cons of governments taking a hand in the stabilization of traded agricultural commodities. World Bank, Washington, D.C. Mimeo.

Sabur, S. A., and Quadat-I-Elahi. 1992. Trend and intertemporal paddy price fluctuation in Bangladesh. *Bangladesh Journal of Agricultural Economics* 16 (December): 60–69.

Sahn, D. E. 1989. Policy recommendations for improving food security. In *Seasonal variability in Third World agriculture: The consequences for food security*, ed. D. E. Sahn. Baltimore, Md., U.S.A.: Johns Hopkins University Press.

Sahn, D. E., and C. Delgado. 1989. The nature and implications for market interventions of seasonal food price variability. In *Seasonal variability in Third World agriculture: The consequences for food security*, ed. D. E. Sahn. Baltimore, Md., U.S.A.: Johns Hopkins University Press.

Salant, S. W. 1983. The vulnerability of price stabilization schemes to speculative attack. *Journal of Political Economy* 91 (1): 1–38.

Sapaun, R. 1989. The development of rice marketing in Indonesia. *Indonesian Food Journal* 1 (1): 21–39.

Sarris, A. 1984. Commodity-price theory and public stabilization stocks. In *Food security: Theory, policy, and perspectives from Asia and the Pacific Rim*, ed. A. H. Chisholm and R. Tyers. Lexington, Mass., U.S.A.: Lexington Books.

Scandizzo, P., P. Hazell, and J. Anderson. 1984. *Risky agricultural markets: Price forecasting and the need for intervention policies*. Boulder, Colo., U.S.A.: Westview Press.

Scheinkman, J. A., and J. Schechtman. 1983. A simple competitive model with production and storage. *Review of Economic Studies* 50 (162): 427–441.

Schiff, M., and A. Valdés. 1992a. *The political economy of agricultural pricing policy*, vol. 4. Baltimore, Md., U.S.A.: Johns Hopkins University Press.

———. 1992b. The effects of intervention on price variability. In *The political economy of agricultural pricing policy*. A World Bank Comparative Study. Baltimore, Md., U.S.A.: Johns Hopkins University Press.

Sen, A. 1991. *Poverty and famines: An essay on entitlement and deprivation*. Oxford: Oxford University Press.

Shahabuddin, Q. 1991. *A disaggregated model for stabilization of rice prices in Bangladesh*. Working Papers on Food Policy in Bangladesh No. 3. Washington, D.C.: International Food Policy Research Institute.

Siamwalla, A. 1986. Approaches to price insurance for farmers. In *Crop insurance for agricultural development*, ed. P. Hazell, C. Pomerada, and A. Valdés. Baltimore, Md., U.S.A.: Johns Hopkins University Press for the International Food Policy Research Institute.

———. 1988. Public stock management. In *Agricultural price policy for developing countries*, ed. J. Mellor and R. Ahmed. Baltimore, Md., U.S.A.: Johns Hopkins University Press for the International Food Policy Research Institute.

Siamwalla, A., and S. Setboonsarng. 1989. *Trade, exchange rate, and agricultural pricing policies in Thailand*. Washington, D.C.: World Bank.

Siamwalla, A., S. Setboonsarng, D. Patmasiriwat, M. Kaosa-ard, and S. Isvilanonda. 1992. *Food situation outlook in Asia: Case study of Thailand*. Thailand Development Research Institute, Thailand.

Sicular, T., ed. 1989. *Food price policy in Asia*. Ithaca, N.Y., U.S.A.: Cornell University Press.

Stiglitz, J. 1987. Some theoretical aspects of agricultural policies. *The World Bank Research Observer* 2 (1): 43–60.

Sudaryanto, T., E. Hermanto, and E. Pasandran. 1992. *Food situation and outlook for Indonesia*. Bogor, Indonesia: Center for Agro-socio Economic Research.

Sukriya, A., A. Sugeng, and S. Milyo. 1989. The role of BULOG in the Indonesian economy. *Indonesian Food Journal* 1 (1).

Thailand, Ministry of Agriculture and Cooperatives, Office of Agricultural Economics. 1991. *Agricultural statistics of Thailand, crop year 1990/91*. Bangkok: Ministry of Agriculture and Cooperatives.

Timmer, P. C. 1988. Agricultural prices and stabilization policy. Harvard Institute for International Development, Cambridge, Mass., U.S.A. Mimeo.

———. 1989a. Food policy: The rationale for government intervention. *Food Policy* 14 (February): 17–27.

———. 1989b. Food price stabilization: Rationale, design, and implementation. Discussion Paper No. 298. Cambridge, Mass., U.S.A.: Harvard University, Harvard Institute for International Development.

———. 1989c. Indonesia's experience with rice market interventions. *Indonesian Food Journal* 1 (1): 48–63.

———. 1993. Rural bias in the East and South East Asian rice economy: Indonesia in comparative perspective. *Journal of Development Studies* 29 (July): 149–176.

Turnovsky, S. J. 1974. Price expectations and welfare gains from price stabilization. *American Journal of Agricultural Economics* 56 (4): 706–716.

———. 1976. The distribution of welfare gains from price stabilization: The case of multiplicative disturbances. *International Economic Review* 17 (1): 133–148.

———. 1978. The distribution of welfare gains from price stabilization: A survey of some theoretical issues. In *Stabilizing world commodity markets*, ed. G. F. Adams and S. A. Klein. Lexington, Mass., U.S.A.: Lexington Books.

Turnovsky, S. J., H. Shalit, and A. Schmitz. 1980. Consumer's surplus, price instability, and consumer welfare. *Econometrica* 48 (1): 135–152.

Tyers, R., and J. Anderson. 1992. *Disarray in world markets: A quantitative assessment.* Cambridge: Cambridge University Press.

Umali, D. 1985. Rice marketing and prices under Philippine government price stabilization. Bureau of Agricultural Economics, Department of Agriculture, the Philippines. Manila.

UNDP (United Nations Development Programme). 1988. *Bangladesh agriculture: Performance and policies.* Bangladesh Agriculture Sector Review. New York.

United Nations. Various years. *Statistical yearbook.* New York.

Unnevehr, L. J. 1985. The costs of squeezing marketing margins: Philippine government intervention in rice markets. *The Developing Economies* 23 (2): 116–136.

Walters, A. A. 1987. The mischief of moving average pricing. World Bank, Washington, D.C. Mimeo.

Waugh, F. 1944. Does the consumer benefit from price instability? *Quarterly Journal of Economics* 57 (4): 602–614.

World Bank. 1990. *Indonesia: Formulating for sustained growth*. Washington, D.C.

————. 1991. *Bangladesh food policy review: Adjusting to the Green Revolution*. Country Department I. Washington, D.C.

————. 1992. *Indonesia: Agricultural transformation challenges and opportunities*, vols. I and II. Country Department III. Washington, D.C.

————. 1993. *Managing policy reforms in the real world—Asian experiences*, ed. G. Lamb and R. Wearing. Washington, D.C.

————. 1994. *Pakistan: A strategy for sustainable agricultural growth*. Washington, D.C.

Wright, B. D., and J. C. Williams. 1982. The economic role of commodity storage. *Economic Journal* 92 (367): 596–614.

————. 1984. The welfare effects of the introduction of storage. *Quarterly Journal of Economics* 99 (1): 169–182.

————. 1988a. Measurement of consumer gains from market stabilization. *American Journal of Agricultural Economics* 70 (3): 617–628.

————. 1988b. The incidence of market stabilizing price support schemes. *Economic Journal* 98 (December): 1183–1198.

————. 1991. *Storage and commodity markets*. Cambridge, U.K.: Cambridge University Press.